NO
FCKS
GIVEN

NO F❤CKS GIVEN

The Zero-Accountability Guide to Getting Over a Boy

Toni Tone

4th ESTATE • *London*

4th Estate
An imprint of HarperCollins*Publishers*
1 London Bridge Street
London SE1 9GF

www.4thestate.co.uk

HarperCollins*Publishers*
Macken House
39/40 Mayor Street Upper
Dublin 1
D01 C9W8
Ireland

First published in Great Britain in 2025 by 4th Estate

1

A catalogue record for this book is
available from the British Library

ISBN 978-0-00-859125-0

Set in Adobe Garamond Pro by Six Red Marbles UK, Thetford, Norfolk

Printed and bound in the UK [using 100% renewable electricity at CPI Group (UK) Ltd]

I'm dedicating this book to my sister, Tara, and my best friend, Carina. We've had many discussions about guys and why they do the sh*t they do. Thanks for trusting me with your feelings. Thanks for encouraging me to be more vulnerable when I share my own feelings. Thanks for being there for me while I navigated my heartbreaks. Little did I know all our discussions would manifest into a book one day.

For all the girls who have had their hearts broken by a boy. This one is also for you.

Contents

Foreword

So, you want to get over a guy? First off, I am so sorry that someone's son has broken your heart. It hurts me to know you felt compelled to order this book in the first place. Don't get me wrong, I'm happy you're reading *No F*cks Given*, but I hate that you were led here by something so traumatic. Break-ups truly suck.

I know this because I've been exactly where you are right now – on more than one occasion. I've had my heart broken at different stages of my life and, each time, I navigated the break-up differently and picked up a few techniques for healing (and coping) along the way. I've also seen heartbreak around me in different forms.

Whether that's friends crying over guys who didn't see their worth, family members going through divorces or simply observing how heartbreak influences storytelling and media. Love is everywhere and, by default, heart-break is everywhere too.

Before I begin helping you, I think it's only fair to briefly mention some of my personal experiences, which I'll go into more as this book continues. Firstly, I want to stress that heartbreak is still possible even when you initiate a break-up. I think this is important to mention because sometimes we leave people not because we want to but because we need to. I've been through break-ups that hurt me, even though I was the one who did the leaving. Sometimes, you leave because you've been disre-spected; other times, it's because you feel yourself shrinking. Maybe you even feel as if you're more invested in the relationship than the other person, so you depart as a means of self-protection. Basically, I admit I walked away sometimes, but that doesn't mean it hurt any less.

Then there are the heartbreaks where you don't do the leaving, but you're left, and it hits you like a ton of bricks. Being left by someone is a real blow to the ego. It can have you questioning why you weren't 'enough' and why they felt comfortable breaking your heart. This type of heartbreak is the type that most people struggle to get over. It's a gut-wrenching pain that brings blows to our self-esteem and leads us to confront some of our most intense thoughts and emotions.

I've called this book *No F*cks Given* for two reasons. The first reason is because, for the first time ever, I'm giving no f*cks about the level of personal details I'm willing to share. You're going to read about my vulnerable moments – like the time I had my heart broken so painfully that my doctor told me it was changing my skin colour. And my slightly unhinged moments – like the time I briefly obsessed over a woman one of my exes cheated on me with. You're going to read about so much more than I've ever shared before.

So, to get back to my experiences. I'm a happily married woman as I write this book, but to get to this point, I went through some sh*t. My first heartbreak was in my early twenties when I was at university. Now, when I started university, I already had a boyfriend, who I had been dating for two years during school. Despite the both of us being so young, he was such a sweet boyfriend to me and our relationship was very loving and healthy. But with the excitement of starting university and being embedded in a new city with new people, I ended the relationship. In hindsight, I did it cruelly. After about two weeks of being at university and barely replying to his messages, I broke up with him via text message. At the time, so many things ran through my mind. For one, I knew he wanted us to lose our virginities to each other once I finally started university and I just wasn't ready for that. Then to top it all off, there were boys everywhere, and at 18, I was excited at the thought of starting something new, as a 'grown-up' (funny how we think we're grown when we're 18). I couldn't bring myself to verbally explain why I wanted to end it, so the text message gave me an easy way out. Looking back, it was such an awful thing to do because I basically blindsided him. From memory, his reaction to it was weirdly calm. Nonchalant even. But deep down, I knew he was hurting and acting like he was unbothered was his way of coping. In this situation, I was the heartbreaker, and not long after that, I started dating a new guy. Let's call him Mr What-Was-I-Thinking. In hindsight, some might say Mr What-Was-I-Thinking may have been my karma for breaking the heart of my teenage love, but nobody deserves karma like the relationship I experienced.

When I met Mr What-Was-I-Thinking, I was 18. I was drawn in by his charisma; he had a bit of a cheeky personality that was admittedly quite intriguing to me. He also seemed a little rough around the edges compared to what I was used to, as he was a bit of a 'bad boy'. You know the type. They're usually magnetic, very rebellious, popular with the ladies and known to break the law sometimes. As someone who had never dated a bad boy before, I was infatuated. The more I got to know him, the more I was given access to his softer side. He would rush to the university canteen in the mornings to fetch me breakfast before lectures; he would leave me little notes in the form of makeshift treasure hunts – and at the time, words of affirmation were the key to my heart, so hearing him express how much he liked me pretty much sealed the deal for me. I think the young me felt flattered at the thought of his willingness to be gentle with me. Before I knew it, we were boyfriend and girlfriend and everything seemed to be going great . . . until it wasn't.

One day, I met up with my friends. Mr What-Was-I-Thinking and I had been together for just under a year and things seemed to be going well. I'd go as far as saying that, at the time, I felt as if I was in love with him. Looking back, I know it was more infatuation than anything but, as a teenager, I struggled to know the difference.

As I walked towards my friends, I recall seeing a look of worry on their faces that I had never seen before. 'Toni, you're going to wanna hear this . . .,' one of them said.

One of my girlfriends had gone to a special dinner and, at this dinner, the girls in attendance got to talking about guys they liked at university. One of the girls at the dinner shared a story about an intimate encounter she had had with a guy – a guy who happened to have the exact same name as my boyfriend. This may not sound incredibly alarming, but my boyfriend's name was quite unique, so it was easy for my friend to determine that the girl was indeed talking about him. I was distraught. I felt like the wool had been pulled over my eyes, and there was a knot in my stomach as if my body was gearing up to vomit the shame and disgust away. But with that said, I'm notoriously good at playing unbothered, so I don't think the true scale of my disappointment came across to my friends at the time. Part of the reason why I kept my true feelings in was because I felt embarrassed and I didn't want anyone to know how deep the shame went. In my mind, if I acted unbothered, then the embarrassment of the situation wouldn't be so obvious. I also didn't want it to appear like another person – let alone a guy – could have that much of an emotional impact on me. As an older sister, I'm typically the level-headed, strong-minded person in my friendship groups. I just didn't want to look 'broken' to anyone. I remember cussing Mr What-Was-I-Thinking out to my girls and informing them that I would be confronting him the following day. When the time came, I told him I knew about everything. He attempted to lie about it, but I refused to budge. During his attempts at lying, I felt so frustrated. It's one thing to do something to hurt me, but then to act like I'm stupid? The gaslighting drove me crazy. In the end, with water in his eyes, he came clean. He also stressed that he loved me, it meant nothing and he couldn't lose me. What do you think 19-year-old me did? I forgave him.

Have you ever been in a position where you swore you would never forgive a man for cheating on you, but eventually did? As a teenager I was so sure that I would never take a guy back after he had broken my trust, so when I forgave Mr What-Was-I-Thinking, I felt deeply ashamed and embarrassed – particularly because my friends had knowledge of our relationship and his misdeeds. At the time, I remember asking myself why I was willing to progress with the relationship. The answer? I truly believed I loved him and he loved me. I also believed that he meant it when he said he would never hurt me again – but boy was I wrong about that.

For the next three years, the relationship was a constant rollercoaster of ups and downs. Mr What-Was-I-Thinking would do something to hurt me, then beg for forgiveness and offer up a gesture in an attempt to reel me back in. One time, I got tickets to see Chris Brown (this was before his 2009 assault) and I was so excited because I was a huge fan back then.

The hurtful things Mr What-Was-I-Thinking did included punching walls in anger, breaking my things, lying and, eventually, cheating again. At the time, I didn't regard his behaviour as abusive. Instead, I naively put it down to him having anger problems. It was only years later that I was able to acknowledge that his controlling, manipulative and aggressive tendencies were indeed forms of domestic abuse. But I still, even then, mentally separated domestic abuse from domestic violence. For whatever reason, I was under the impression that I hadn't been a victim of domestic violence because he had never hit me. It wasn't until I was 30 that I learnt that breaking things around a person in a threatening or aggressive manner also constituted domestic violence because violence includes action which creates an environment of fear and intimidation and causes destruction, pain or suffering.

For context, I remember a day when we were driving around London. Well, he was driving – and I was in the passenger seat. We were at the Marble Arch roundabout and a cyclist cut him off. Instead of letting it go, Mr What-Was-I-Thinking proceeded to exit the car, hurl insults at the cyclist, pick up the cyclist's bike and throw it as far as he could. I remember sitting in the car feeling disgusted as I watched him struggle to manage his anger. On his return to the car, we had a conversation about his behaviour; he didn't like my disapproval of it. As we drove towards Soho, I remember him getting angrier and angrier. He wanted to release all the pent-up anger inside him, so he stopped the car, jumped out, walked to the nearest phone box and punched it. It wasn't one of the popular red phone boxes tourists take photos in: it was one of the old glass BT phone boxes. I remember hearing the impact of his punch and seeing the pane of glass on the phone box shatter. Upon realisation of what he had done, he jumped back into the car and sped off towards university. I was so frightened that I sat in silence through the whole trip – peering at his glass-cut hand that was dripping with blood. I kept quiet because

I knew he was angry and I didn't want to make him angrier.

Not long after this, I discovered that earlier on in the relationship, he had also had sex with an ex-girlfriend. I felt like such an idiot for forgiving him the first time and falling victim to his disloyalty yet again. In the end, the relationship was too much of a burden for me. After years of dealing with his temper and constant lying, I finally decided enough was enough and made the brave decision to walk away. Want to know the sickest part about it for me, though? I was still sad! I know, I know – he was a scumbag to me, so why was I hurt? I think a lot of my sadness was tied to disappointment. Disappointment about his behaviour and the relationship I felt I deserved but didn't receive. Heartbreak is annoyingly complicated (which I'll go into more later). Before we ever experience it, we can assume it only occurs when we lose someone who was good to us. But no, losing someone *we* cared for, whether they cared about us or not, still hurts.

Have you ever been mistreated by someone but because you care for them so much, you make excuses for them? That was me in university. I made excuses for Mr What-Was-I-Thinking's anger, for his lying, for his total disregard for my feelings. It was a mess. When I think about that relationship as a woman in her mid-thirties, I can't help but feel shocked that I put up with a lot of his behaviour. The girl I was then is so far removed from the woman I am today but, without that experience, I wouldn't have gained the wisdom I have now – I guess I'm grateful for that.

My second heartbreak was Mr Dismissive Avoidant. This heartbreak was hands down my toughest adult heartbreak – partially because, at the time, I didn't think the relationship would end with a broken heart. I told myself he was the guy I was going to end up marrying. Why? I think it was because we'd been together for many years, we'd met each other's families and he reminded me of my dad in a few ways – so he felt . . . relatable. As I'm typing this, I'm laughing to myself because I paused or ended that relationship so many times. 'Let's go on a break', 'I can't do this anymore', 'I'm not happy', 'I don't love you.' I said it all – whether I meant it or not.

I met Mr Dismissive Avoidant when I was 23. At the time, I was still recovering from the emotional damage I had experienced at the hands of Mr What-Was-I-Thinking, so when Mr Dismissive Avoidant asked for my number, I informed him that I didn't want to share it with him as I wasn't looking for a relationship. But, with me being a millennial, I told him that he could add me on Facebook instead. He added me and sent me a message, but I didn't reply. Almost a year later, he wrote to me again but this time round, I was in a better head space, so I replied and took him up on his request for a date. We ended up going to a restaurant where, eventually, we found ourselves taking part in some karaoke. The date was enjoyable – one date turned into two, which turned into three and more. He lived in a different city, so I'd spend weekends with him in the flat he and his mother rented – although his mother was living in a different country at the time, so he was sharing the flat with a housemate. He didn't have a car, which meant I'd leave my parents' house to take a bus to the coach station, then sit through a 90-minute coach journey, then get on the train to meet him. Looking back, I must have really liked him, because why the hell was I embarking on a three-hour odyssey to see a guy who wasn't my boyfriend? I'm cringing at the thought of it right now. At this time in our story, sex was off the table because I had a rule: I'd only have sex with a guy if we were in a committed relationship. We spent about five months dating until I asked the dreaded 'What are we?' question (a question I now tell women never to ask).

When you ask a guy, 'What are we?', it can imply that defining the relationship is solely his decision – that he holds the power to label what you are. This can create a dynamic where you're waiting for him to validate the relationship, rather than engaging as an equal. A healthier approach is to have an open, mutual conversation about how each of you feels and where things are heading. From that dialogue, you can decide for yourself whether the relationship aligns with what you want and whether it's worth continuing or walking away. After I asked Mr Dismissive Avoidant 'What are we?', he replied with a spiel about how he wasn't looking for a relationship. Isn't that strange? Men will hit on you, ask you out, take you on dates, prompt you to catch feelings and then tell you they aren't looking for a relationship. Like . . . you're the one who chased me! I remember feeling dumbfounded. There I was, channelling *Around the World in Eighty Days* to spend time with this guy in a different city and he didn't even want anything serious. 'At least you didn't sleep with him,' I told myself, as a means of psychological comfort.

I was so insulted that I stopped seeing and conversing with Mr Dismissive Avoidant until he reached out again a month later, telling me he missed me. I thought that perhaps he'd changed his mind about not wanting to be in a relationship and, just like clockwork, we were dating again. A few weeks into us reconnecting, I asked him the same 'What are we?' question and, unsurprisingly, I received the same answer. I was livid. 'How dare he reel me back in – only to waste my time,' I thought. I ended up cutting off all communication with him and telling myself, 'I should have believed him the first time.'

After the second attempt at dating him ended, I didn't hear from Mr Dismissive Avoidant. That is, until a bouquet arrived at my workplace with my name on the card two months later. I had butterflies in my stomach, though I tried to squash them as I picked up the notecard to read it. 'Will you be my girlfriend?' A burst of glee washed over me, along with a naive sense of pride and self-satisfaction. 'Wow! I must be amazing,' I thought. Mr Anti-Commitment was willing to commit just because I didn't speak to him for two months. I recall texting my best friend, who was just as shocked as me. Once my working day had ended, I got in touch with Mr Dismissive Avoidant and attempted to play it cool, but the truth is I was so happy. I really liked him.

Eventually, the relationship grew into years of us

being together. Six and a half years, to be exact. It even lasted through a whole relocation when Mr Dismissive Avoidant moved abroad two years into our relationship. Although, when I say it lasted six and a half years, there's a caveat – this relationship was an on-again, off-again cycle.

Have you ever broken up with someone because you loved them deeply and wanted them to act right? In your head, you think the break-up will trigger a massive transformation in them, but that rarely happens. When it came to Mr Dismissive Avoidant, I used to ask for breaks regularly. Even though he wasn't an unkind boyfriend or terrible boyfriend, he wasn't a great one either. He was just kinda 'there'. He got away with doing the bare minimum – just enough that I wouldn't complain, but not enough that I'd feel secure. The same commitment phobia he displayed at the beginning of the relationship echoed throughout it – and this would lead to a lack of fulfilment in me. For the most part, being with him felt like going nowhere, slowly, and I would signal my frustrations by initiating time away from each other.

One thing about that man, though, he knew what to say to get me back and I loved him, so I listened. At one point during the relationship, I deceived myself into thinking we'd always find a way back to each other because it was meant to be – but that wasn't it. He was an avoidant and my previous relationship had left me with an anxious attachment style. The thing about avoidants and anxiously attached people is that they often fall into a push-pull dynamic that creates a break-up and makeup cycle. Their attachment styles trigger each other's deepest fears and the cycle ends up looking something like this: The avoidant attempts to avoid commitment because they value independence and fear being overwhelmed by too much emotional closeness. The anxious partner craves emotional closeness and therefore seeks reassurance but that can make an avoidant feel suffocated and pull away, which in turn makes the anxious person worry. This only creates problems which eventually trigger a break-up by either party. However, as much as avoidants may fear commitment, they can also experience loneliness due to the limited emotional bonds they create in life and a fear of being alone often leads them to reconnect with their anxiously attached partner when they desire comfort. Their anxiously attached partner – who is likely anxious because they've been hurt or abandoned in the past – fears further abandonment and subsequently overlooks the avoidant's behaviour to rebuild and reconcile. However, if neither party has done the necessary work on themselves, they fall into the same cycle all over again – a desire for reassurance and a feeling of suffocation.

I'd see incremental improvements in Mr Dismissive Avoidant's behaviour every time we reconnect, but nothing that erased the discontentment in me. However, there was one break that didn't come with an incremental improvement – the break-up I initiated before the final breakdown of the relationship. We had been together for five years and there was no real discussion happening about the future. Every time I would bring it up, I sensed discomfort, so I decided to call it quits. The push and pull cycle commenced and we were back together not too long afterwards – but there was a coldness and nonchalance about him that I'd never seen before. He also made it clear that during the break-up, he had been with other women – something I hadn't heard from him previously. I remember feeling deeply concerned. Was it my fault? Did I bite off more than I could chew? Did I make a mistake by breaking up with him this time?

Things felt different once we got back together. I felt as

if there was significant emotional distance between us. It all eventually ended after my thirtieth birthday. I flew to Bali with him, my mother, my sister and my best friend. We had an amazing trip together and, on my birthday, he gifted me with a card and £1,000. At the time, it was the most money I'd ever been given by a guy and I was so thankful. We watched a birthday montage my best friend put together for me and his eyes welled up as he took it in. In the card, he wrote that he loved me, that I was beautiful on the inside and outside, that anyone who knows me is lucky to have me in their life and so much more . . . one week later, he told me marriage was something he didn't want for himself – so that was it for us. Six and a half years down the drain.

This break-up deeply hurt me because, at one point, I thought that relationship would be my last. After all, like I shared earlier, we had met each other's families and we had been in each other's lives through new jobs, births, deaths, relocations and so much more. And with every break-up, we always reconnected. Walking away from the longest love I'd experienced at that time shattered me.

I'm writing this book because, as you can tell by now, I've been on heartbreak journeys – maybe even similar to the ones you have found yourself on – and I have learned several things along the way that have helped me to survive, as well as thrive. I want to be your voice of comfort during this time because I know how desperately I needed comfort when I was going through my own heartbreaks. I want to provide advice that will help you move on. But I want to do it in the most matter-of-fact way that I've ever written.

This is the second reason this book is called *No F*cks Given*. I want you to give not one single f*ck about feeling hurt right now. I want you to feel all the feels, from the slightly painful to the deeply gut-wrenching. Why? Because you have to feel to heal and I want you to do so unapologetically. It might hurt, but that short-term pain will be long-term gain and it's a big part of why I think women handle heartbreak better than men. The immediate processing that we are typically willing to undertake, which has us quickly feeling angry, sad, ashamed, lonely, and worried, is ironically helpful to us because it encourages us to initiate healing earlier. Delaying emotional responses and dismissing our feelings only contributes to an array of challenges further down the line. So, I want you to feel all your emotions, from start to finish, and when you feel the negative ones, I want you to administer zero accountability.

At this point, you're probably thinking, 'Why zero accountability?' In my first book, *I Wish I Knew This Earlier*, I was loud about accountability on your journey towards dating, loving and healing. But there is a time, place and mood for holding yourself accountable. Administer zero accountability when it comes to thinking about the needs and wants of past men in your life, but be accountable to yourself for your own happiness and fulfilment because, right now, nobody can make you happier than you can. I want this book to be the book you read when you've tried all the gentle healing practices that, for whatever reason, don't seem to be working for you. I want this book to be the book you gift your friends when they're still hung up over a no-good man and can't seem to move on. I want this book to be the book you run to when you just want to scream, 'What a d*ck!' Jokes aside, I do believe that there are situations where actively disregarding accountability can be helpful, especially in the emotional aftermath of heartbreak. For one, break-ups can be devastating and self-blame can worsen mental health. When you reject accountability, you shield yourself from unnecessary guilt and preserve your self-esteem.

Additionally, society typically doesn't hold men to the

same standards as women, especially in relationships. I often hear people say things like 'she can't keep a man' after a woman's relationship ends – but rarely anything suggesting the man wasn't worth keeping. If guys are allowed to say, 'I wanted something different', 'It just wasn't working for me' or 'I wasn't ready for a relationship' without deep self-reflection, why should women carry the emotional burden of holding themselves accountable and unpacking everything? Society often pressures women to reflect on things they could have changed or done to keep a relationship going. Applying zero accountability counteracts this gendered emotional labour and rejects the idea that women must always 'fix themselves' to keep a man or get another. If men can move on without deep self-reflection about their actions and choices, then why can't we? Women are expected to unpack everything, grow and evolve . . . but sometimes, we're not the problem! Sometimes, the man really was the problem and trying to take accountability where none is needed gaslights us into believing we had more control than we actually did.

Zero accountability encourages us to let go of situations that were never meant to work instead of forcing unnecessary self-reflection. When accountability is removed, validation comes from self-love, not dissecting mistakes. Instead of thinking, 'What could I have done differently?', your mindset shifts to 'I deserve more . . . I deserve better.' Stripping yourself of accountability as you read this book will encourage you to move on from the past without romanticising it. It will also help you to feel the full spectrum of your emotions without blaming yourself in the process. One thing about applying too much personal accountability is that it can lead you to exaggerate your own role in a break-up while minimising the other person's. Also, in assessing how you navigated the past, you remain entangled in it. Zero accountability helps you cut the cord without self-blame. Why obsess over your role in a relationship that is already over?

I'm not disputing that accountability has its place – sometimes we do need to take ownership for our sh*t – but I also believe there are instances where it's perfectly fine to reject accountability. Particularly when someone has done something that is undeniably uncaring, inconsiderate, hurtful or malicious. I don't consider applying accountability when I think back to the time Mr What-Was-I-Thinking punched a public phone box and left himself bloodied afterwards. As far as I'm concerned, that had everything to do with his lack of emotional intelligence – and nothing to do with me. Zero account-ability can help you heal faster, preserve your self-worth and avoid unnecessary self-blame. Sometimes, the healthiest move isn't self-reflection, it's allowing yourself to move on without looking back.

Experience has taught me that recovering from heart-break is a process that is filled with many ups and downs. You'll have days where you wake up and feel angry, or days where you feel distraught, unable to think, eat or sleep as normal. You'll have days where you feel lonely, ashamed or even nostalgic. But then you'll have days where you wake up and suddenly feel as if you're coping and everything is under control. Then a bad day could creep up on you all over again . . . I've written this book with that in mind. I want this book to touch on the array of emotions one might feel while dealing with a broken heart. I also know that this book might not be something you read once, or even twice. You may choose to return to it whenever you feel a certain feeling. You may choose to read the chapters in a totally random order. Do what-ever suits you and the journey you're on.

Healing from a traumatic experience is difficult and can often feel isolating, but this book is my way of letting you know that you're not alone and you're living through an experience shared by countless people – including me. As a bonus, I also called this book *No F*cks Given* because I'm hoping that by the end of it, you will give much less of a f*ck about the guy who broke your heart.

And on that note, let's begin.

Anger

I bet you're angry. I would be if I was you.

Were you lied to? Were you cheated on? Were you deceived? I want you to give yourself the permission to experience an emotion society often wants women to dull – and that's anger.

Anger is often one of the first emotions people feel after heartbreak because it's a natural defence mechanism against the pain of loss. In fact, even when people experience bereavement, the five stages of grief outline experiencing anger before depression. When a relationship ends in an abrupt or unfair way, anger provides us with a sense of power in a situation that may feel unstable.

It's a natural response to broken expectations and reinforces the fact that painful emotions are justified, rather than allowing feelings of guilt or self-blame to take over. Anger serves a purpose.

When people hurt us, it's normal to feel indignation. It's normal to feel resentful. It's normal to want revenge. I don't want you to feel bad for feeling these feelings. I want you to accept the fact that you feel them and accept the fact that it's not your fault that you're angry. Because a lack of acceptance of these difficult emotions will only make them spiral – and we don't want that. In fact, if I'm being honest with you, anger was one emotion I felt more than any other emotion after a break-up. Immediately after my relationship with Mr What-Was-I-Thinking ended, I felt so angry at him for all the lying, deceit, cheating and aggression I endured. I felt angry at him for thinking it was okay to treat me the way he did. I felt angry when I saw his face or even heard his name. I was full of anger.

Society often paints a picture that tells women they should be graceful after a break-up. People often encourage forgiveness, accountability and moving on quietly – but why is anger in women discouraged when it's one of the most natural responses to betrayal and heartbreak? Please allow yourself to rebel against this societal expectation by feeling your anger – and do this with the understanding that anger comes first because it protects you from immediate emotional collapse. Your anger will give you the strength to process the situation before deeper emotions like sadness kick in, and it's important for you to process your anger because, despite what people say, anger can be such a strong catalyst for healing when administered in the right way.

Speaking for myself, I am much less likely to wallow when I'm angry because anger propels me into action. When I allow myself to be angry, I'm less consumed by self-blaming thoughts and more consumed by feelings of self-worth. The sad me thinks, 'Was it my fault?', while the angry me says, 'I'm too good for him!' What is your anger telling you? Let it out or write it down if that would be helpful.

When you're angry, you're also less likely to romanticise the past and make excuses for bad behaviour because you hold the right person accountable and you acknowledge the disrespect, the broken promises, the lies, the betrayal. When you're angry, you're less likely to forget – which acts as a natural defence mechanism against nostalgia. Anger is a powerful reminder of why you need to move on.

'Hell hath no fury like a woman scorned' is a popular saying that has been heard throughout history – in theatre, movies, books and more. It is a paraphrased line from a seventeenth-century play by English playwright William Congreve, called *The Mourning Bride*. The full quote reads:

'Heaven has no rage like love to hatred turned, nor hell a fury like a woman scorned.'

This line is one of Congreve's most famous and it captures the intense and sometimes vengeful emotions that can emerge from a woman after she has been betrayed and heartbroken. In my opinion, this statement rings true – for both women *and* men. We've seen examples of this play out in real life and in media, whether it's the late Lisa 'Left Eye' Lopez, who set fire to her boyfriend's mansion in 1994 after an argument over allegations of infidelity, the 2014 movie *Gone Girl*, which saw Amy, played by Rosamund Pike, fake her own death and frame her husband for murder after discovering he cheated, or singers Carrie Underwood and Jazmine Sullivan penning songs about destroying an ex-partner's car after experiencing betrayal. Hurt people hurt people.

Society acts like anger is always a 'negative' emotion

and while those examples of post-heartbreak anger are pretty extreme, anger also serves a purpose and it's a sign a person is emotionally in tune. It's a sign a person cares about themselves and can acknowledge when one of their boundaries has been disrespected. Anger is normal to feel and the only time it *is* negative is when it's coupled with actions that can be detrimental to your safety and wellbeing or the safety and wellbeing of others.

After taking Mr What-Was-I-Thinking back at 19, I remember how badly I wanted him to feel the magnitude of the hurt that he had caused me. So much so that part of me wanted to pretend that everything was fine and then cheat back. I'm not going to lie to you, I did try. While we were together, I started talking to a guy I met on a night out with friends: Mr Oxford. I thought he was intelligent and good looking but, ultimately, our conversation was triggered by my underlying thirst for revenge. Mr Oxford was my 'get back' guy, which is likely why that situation didn't manifest into anything. I dabbled in retaliation but, despite all my efforts, I was ridden with guilt. I just couldn't bring myself to progress things any further than simply talking. At the time, I remember being annoyed at myself for not being able to 'cheat properly'. My continued care for Mr What-Was-I-Thinking, coupled with my moral compass, really pissed me off.

I'm sure some of you can relate to this. Maybe not even in the context of relationships, perhaps even when it comes to your friends. Has someone ever hurt you to the point you wanted to hurt them in the exact same way back, but you just couldn't bring yourself to be a total b*tch? Then you felt frustrated that the b*tch in you was that considerate? I have battled my inner b*tch so many times and my kind inner voice usually wins. In hindsight, I'm glad for it – because the truth is, you should never compromise your character to prove a lesson to people who aren't even worth your time or energy. Put simply, don't let a f*ck boy change you from a good person to an awful one. While anger is a normal emotion, it's about how you handle the anger that makes a difference. The anger I felt almost drove me to do something that I know I would have later regretted, but in the end, I considered how it might impact my personal wellbeing. I could have also destroyed Mr What-Was-I-Thinking's belongings like Bernadine in the movie *Waiting to Exhale*, but if he had decided to get the police involved that could have impacted my life in a detrimental way. So when I say 'zero accountability', there is one caveat. Do not hold yourself accountable for the pain men put you through but do hold yourself accountable when it comes to doing what's in your best interest. Don't embrace feelings of guilt or self-blame, don't beat yourself up for other people's wrongdoings, but DO hold yourself accountable when it comes to prioritising your wellbeing. That's the only time I'm ever going to tell you to exhibit accountability: when it comes to making decisions that could have a massive impact on your safety and quality of life. So no, I'm not suggesting you light up somebody's house like Left Eye or frame your ex for murder like Amy Dunne. But I am suggesting that you allow yourself to feel utterly enraged about the fact you've been heartbroken. If you want to cuss your ex out, do it. If you want to scream down the phone, go for it. If you want to call your girls and let it rip, be my guest. Acknowledge and release the anger. Just don't break the law or do anything that could get you locked up.

One very annoying thing about getting your heart broken by a guy is the fact a part of you still cares about him – maybe even loves him. After being left heart-broken by Mr What-Was-I-Thinking and Mr Dismissive

Avoidant, what grated on me heavily were the lingering thoughts I still had about them. Despite the fact I knew they weren't good for me (for very different reasons). I was angry, but also, I still had feelings for them and I despised that.

I remember watching an episode of *WandaVision* (an American mini-series based on Marvel comics) and I heard a quote that I will never forget: 'What is grief, if not love persevering?' While that message was one of loss and mourning, it emphasised how complicated grief really is. Particularly when it comes to losing someone you love. Heartbreak isn't so different. It's another form of grief. Which is also why we can often feel so angry after it. When we lose someone, it's often followed by feelings of anger and thoughts of 'Why me? Why them?' And like grief, what makes heartbreak extremely painful is the fact the love often perseveres, even when it's undeserved. When we get our heart broken, nobody flicks a switch and prompts us to stop loving and stop caring. We are made to feel unloved, yet at the same time, *we* have not stopped loving. There's a cruelty in that experience. That's one thing about heartbreak that filled me with even more anger and frustration. Why is it that when men are total douchebags to us, we don't immediately discard all feelings for them? I regularly experienced moments where I wished I could just turn my feelings off the second someone did something to hurt or disrespect me. But alas, feelings are complex and getting over someone isn't something that happens overnight.

Outside of feeling angry at Mr What-Was-I-Thinking for breaking my heart, I was also angry at myself for being with Mr What-Was-I-Thinking in the first place. Have you ever dropped your standards to give someone a chance, only for that person to do you dirty? That sh*t is infuriating. Firstly, it's like, how dare they?! How dare they disrespect you when they were the one pushing to be with you in the first place? Secondly, it's maddening because you end up beating yourself up for even settling to begin with. This further affirms the value of applying zero accountability during the healing process. On one hand, someone might say, 'You shouldn't have dated him to begin with', but at the end of the day, when f*ck boys do f*ckery, they do it well. They can be so convincing, so manipulative, so strategic. The 'choose better' rhetoric is a slap in the face after heartbreak because, for many of us, the choice didn't look so bad in the moment! So, in all your anger, please don't be angry at yourself for giving that guy a chance.

Side note: I remember my mum telling me that it's important to be with someone you're attracted to because should they one day annoy you, at least you can look at them and think 'you sexy stupid mother*cker'. If there's zero attraction there, the sight of their face will only anger you even more. Now, that's not to say looks should be the decider when picking a partner. Not at all. There are bigger boxes that people should tick – like shared values, kindness, honesty, etc. That's also not to say you should forgive people for being attractive. Wrongdoing is wrongdoing, and we should all hope our partners don't do anything to disappoint us on a major scale. But with that said, I understand the sentiment my mum was sharing. Long story short, heartbreak comes with a range of complicated emotions already, let alone if you have to talk yourself into dating someone. Being heartbroken by a guy who begged to be with you or who grew on you really does feel like a strong slap in the face. I'm sorry if that's the type of heartbreak you're dealing with right now.

Interestingly, despite my relationship with Mr What-Was-I-Thinking being undisputedly worse than my relationship with Mr Dismissive Avoidant, I emotionally recovered from that relationship a little faster. Unlike with Mr What-Was-I-Thinking, I didn't allow myself to get angry immediately after my break-up with Mr Dismissive Avoidant. Instead, I encouraged myself to bottle my anger up because I assumed it would help me cope. That didn't work, though. I just skipped right over anger and jumped straight into resentment, and one thing about resentment is that it sticks around for much longer!

I believe the resentment I felt at the time was tied to the six and a half years that I had poured into the relationship with Mr Dismissive Avoidant. At one point, I didn't even know what I wanted for myself outside of supporting him and playing 'the dutiful wife in training'. In the end, my efforts were obviously futile, and I felt bitter at the thought of all the years I had lost. I also remember resenting him for feeling like he had strung me along. Remember, this was six and a half years in my twenties, a window of time that society pushes as 'the best years of your life' – at least for women.

Isn't it so sad how society idealises our twenties? Studies on ageism often outline a 'double standard of aging' where men are viewed as aging gracefully, while women are viewed as having more societal value and attractiveness in their youth. This widely shared societal belief is a big reason why so many women rush to get things done 'by thirty'. I admittedly used to be one of these women, so you can imagine how I felt once we had broken up. I really thought this man had stolen the best years of my life, that it was time I had wasted by investing into him and not myself – time that I could have used to chase my dreams or even find someone who was as committed to me as I was to them. In addition, I had so many unmet expectations, which didn't help, and I resented his seemingly nonchalant approach to things. But in the spirit of zero accountability, it wasn't my fault. Society had brainwashed me into believing my twenties would be my best years and, therefore, society gets the blame.

But of course, I didn't know this at the time, and as a result, your girl was resentful. You see, Mr Dismissive Avoidant was someone who seemed to value career and acquiring 'success' more than anything else. He was also someone who was very vocal about the fact I didn't have much of either. I don't believe he ever meant to be malicious when he'd mention my lack of entrepreneurial vision at the time, but it hurt. And I also noticed that the more 'successful' he became, the more distant and superficial he appeared to me. So, when it came to actioning my resentment, what do you think I did? It lit a fire in me that pushed me to focus on outperforming him. I know, I know . . . it sounds childish when I think about it now, especially as I no longer feel so bitter and would only wish well for him – but back then, I didn't give a f*ck. That's my truth and I don't want to lie to you. After that break-up, I took on a mentality of 'I'll show him! You wait!'

It would be disingenuous to say he didn't still have a hold on me after the break-up. He did, otherwise I wouldn't have felt a desire to prove anything to him. As long as we are resentful, it's because we cared, or maybe still do – and caring is nothing to be ashamed of, but we must accept it for what it is. If a break-up is able to bring out a painful emotion in you, it's because your heart was in it at one point.

'Holding on to resentment is like drinking poison and waiting for the other person to die.'

Unfortunately, this quote has been attributed to so many different people that I can't definitively tell you who came up with it, but I wanted to include it anyway because it's the truth. Resentment is a feeling that can easily grow if left unresolved, and while anger may serve a purpose, allowing it to evolve into unchecked resentment can lead to deep hatred, low mood, permanent damage to relationships and even damage to one's health. The most annoying thing about resentment is that it only really affects one person – the person holding on to it. Do you think Mr Dismissive Avoidant was impacted by my ruminating about my success versus his? Absolutely not. I was the only person holding bitterness in my heart. I was the only person being emotionally impacted.

This is why I'm encouraging you to release your anger. For many, resentment is the result of unconfronted anger, anger that has grown to an uncontrollable level. I think part of the reason I felt resentful towards Mr Dismissive Avoidant was due to not allowing myself to truly feel my anger in the first place, and that's why I have come to realise how important it is to let yourself 'feel'. After my break-up, I pretended like everything was okay and, subsequently, any feelings of anger evolved into resentment. Once resentment has kicked in, you are contributing emotional energy to the other person, which only gives them power. Despite my resentment being channelled into things that helped me feel 'successful', the truth is, I was giving Mr Dismissive Avoidant power by centring him in some of my decisions – whether he knew it or not. After all, resenting someone is a form of dwelling. When you hold on to negative memories and feelings, it chips away at your health (which I'll go into in more detail later). Allowing yourself to accept your anger and release it is one way you can free yourself of any resentment, which is truly a gift, as it's a fast track towards healing. Eventually, over time, you will focus less on other people and the pain they caused. Acknowledging your anger is another way of giving yourself permission to accept your truth and inevitably move on.

Eventually, I paid attention to how resentment was impacting me and how in centring Mr Dismissive Avoidant in my career endeavours, I was preventing myself from healing properly. I had to accept the past for what it was, so instead, I reframed the narrative. 'Stop doing things to prove a point to him. Start doing things to prove a point to yourself.' So, my point to you is don't try to numb the pain. Feel the anger. Getting past the pain is the first step towards healing and you can't get past it without acknowledging it. Don't let it grow into resentment and, if it already has grown, accept the way you're feeling and allow yourself to be angry about it. Despite what people might suggest, you're entitled to be angry if you were hurt and you shouldn't feel embarrassed about it because how dare he? How f*cking dare he?

Sadness

One minute, you're angry; the next, you're in tears. That power surge from feeling our anger can be very short-lived.

After experiencing post-heartbreak anger, it's common for sadness to follow. Anger typically acts as the protective shield, allowing us to focus on injustice rather than sitting in the pain of loss. It's often pitched as a lack of control, yet ironically, anger is an emotion which has always provided me with a sense of control, making it easier to distance myself from feelings of sadness. However, the reality of break-ups is that beneath all the anger, there's a whole lot of sadness there – and that's normal.

Speaking for myself, sadness is a more uncomfortable emotion than anger to address, largely because it's an emotion which is often painted as a weakness. The 'sad girl' trope is one that is regularly mocked and sometimes viewed as pathetic (think Bridget in *Bridget Jones' Diary*). In a culture obsessed with moving on and 'glowing up', we can find that pop culture idolises stoic women who appear seemingly unbothered by the misdeeds of men. While bossing up after a break-up is aspirational for many women, you mustn't dismiss your sadness.

We often don't consider the severity of post-break-up symptoms in everyday life because break-ups are so common. But the reality is, after a break-up, most people struggle. Whether that's struggling to go to work or even do everyday tasks like sleep, eat or simply get out of bed. Yet we're often quick to brush this off as 'awww, she's just going through a break-up', without considering the serious mental health implications tied to heartbreak. I, for one, have experienced a mental health shift after a break-up. While I didn't have depression, I experienced anxiety. I believe my anxiety was heavily triggered by a change in routine and uncertainty about what the future held. When you go from talking to the same person every day and planning a future in your head with that person to never talking to them again and that future disappearing, it's very easy to feel restless and nervous. The questions in my mind that often fed feelings of uneasiness included 'What will starting again look like? Will I ever find love again? What do I do now? How do I stop feeling so sh*tty?' I imagine that for many people, the sadness and depression that may occur after a break-up likely stem from the same reasons. Sadness fed my anxiety in a way that had me dwelling on the past and worrying about the future. It had me waking up in the middle of the night because my body refused to relax. It had me missing meals because I felt nauseous for no real reason. It had me procrastinating and missing work deadlines because I couldn't bring myself to do much of anything. All I could think about was how I was feeling and why I was feeling that way.

As well as the routine change and uncertainty about the future, another potential reason we feel sad might be the facing of 'rejection' if the break-up was initiated by the other person. One 2019 study, published in *The Journal of Personality and Social Psychology*, looked into how rejection can impact people's self-esteem and mood. Researchers determined that romantic rejection leads to an array of negative emotions that impact wellbeing. Individuals in the study who were rejected romantically reported feelings of guilt, sadness, anger, shame, loneliness, jealousy, embarrassment and social anxiety. According to the conclusions of the study, these negative emotions can lead to significant distress – potentially contributing to depressive episodes – especially in cases of severe rejection after a break-up.

Feeling sad after a break-up doesn't mean you're weak. Like anger, it is a natural human response to grief. Sadness after a break-up is not a sign that you're emotionally unstable or crazy either. It's simply a sign that you've been impacted by someone you cared for deeply. It's a fundamental emotional response to loss or unmet expectations. It's your mind's way of helping you make sense of your experiences, because after all, that's required to help you eventually move forward. When you skip over sadness, it can have a serious impact on your wellbeing, because unconfronted sadness doesn't disappear. Like anger, it only accumulates. Think of dismissing your sadness like shaking a soda bottle. Every time you dismiss your sadness, you're shaking it. The more you dismiss, the more you shake until, eventually, the bottle explodes. It pays to confront your sadness, despite what people around you might say. When you skip over your sadness, you also risk gaslighting yourself, taking on a very unhelpful accountability approach. In attempting to dismiss how you truly feel, you fall into the risk of blaming yourself for being 'too emotional'. Remember, your sadness is not a problem you have brought on yourself, it's the result of someone hurting you.

On a biological level, when you experience loss, your brain lowers the production of good chemicals like serotonin and dopamine to help your body slow down so you can process what has happened. Anger fuels action and sadness encourages us to understand our experiences and build resilience. When you're left to process the finality of a break-up, that's when the sadness kicks in. This shift is part of the natural healing process that brings clarity; it helps to reveal the needs we suppressed and the problems we encountered. Consider why you feel sad with the knowledge that your sadness also serves a purpose. It's a reminder of your pain and, with time, it will eventually bring you insight.

As natural as sadness is, I'd be lying if I said I didn't hate how impactful it can be on our bodies – emotionally, mentally and physically. I remember how my body changed after my first real heartbreak. Yes – my body.

After finding out Mr What-Was-I-Thinking had cheated on me, I was angry, then distraught. I didn't comprehend the full extent of the impact of that heartbreak on my body until I started noticing small white spots developing on my skin. I already had vitiligo – a condition characterised by the loss of melanin in areas of the skin, which leads to very light or white patches, mostly restricted to a small patch on the shin of my left leg. I developed it as a child but it had laid dormant for almost a decade. After the cheating came to light, I began noticing new spots appearing on my thigh, my back and my neck. Initially, I thought the timing was purely the result of bad luck, until I went to the doctor and learned that psychological stress can contribute to the development or growth of vitiligo. I couldn't believe it.

When we feel sad or stressed, our bodies release hormones, with the primary hormone being cortisol. In healthy doses, cortisol can be helpful. However, too much cortisol is linked to hypertension, hair loss, gastro-intestinal issues, weight gain, skin changes and so much more. It's therefore unsurprising that the side effects of too much cortisol in the body are also common symptoms of heartbreak. Perhaps you have also noticed physical changes when you're going through a break-up?

For my best friend, it's chest pain and pain in her arm. For my sister, it's a twitchy eye. If you pay enough attention, there's likely an obvious physical change in your body that takes place when you're feeling sad and stressed. These changes are our body's way of telling us to take it easy, to take a break or to leave a situation we're in. Pay attention to your body.

People often regard me as someone who is quite laid back. Admittedly, I try not to get hung up over things I can't control. I'm someone who makes a conscious effort to stay calm and rational in times of crisis – and it's largely because of what I went through with Mr What-Was-I-Thinking. The vitiligo spread because, with him, I tried to skip past my sadness. It was largely because I had taken him back, so in my mind, being outwardly sad was ridiculous. But in pretending I was okay, the sadness I felt was only magnified. When I realised that stress had the potential to change my body to such a degree, I made a promise to myself to never allow anybody's dusty son to stress me out to that extent again – and part of that promise to myself involved confronting my sadness head-on.

When I look at my neck or see the spot on my thigh, I'm reminded of what stress can do and because of that,

I'm reminded that I must try my best to manage it – and of course, release it – supporting my belief that releasing emotions, whether anger or sadness, is a must. For some people, giving themselves the freedom to cry is the answer; for others, it's journaling or talking to a friend. Whatever you need to do, do it, because the longer you let the sadness live in you without acknowledging it, the more detrimental the impact on your body. In hindsight, I wish I didn't put up such a front to my friends or Mr What-Was-I-Thinking, but I want you to learn from my own mistake. If you want to be a sad girl, be a sad girl – just do it with zero accountability.

Zero accountability is an important part of confronting your sadness because it prevents you from ruminating over your part in someone else's failure to love you properly. You're sad right now, but not because you're useless or you failed at something. You're sad because your heart was broken by somebody. When you take a zero-accountability approach to sadness, you feel it without over-apologising, over-explaining or dismissing your feelings to make other people feel comfortable. In all your sadness, stop focusing on what you could have done differently in your relationship and channel that sadness into acknowledging what you experienced and how it affected you. If people around you are implying you need to just 'get over it', remember that you are not accountable for anyone else's comfort but your own. You don't owe anyone emotional calmness or a graceful narrative about your experience. If you're sad, be sad, and let people around you know that policing your sadness is unfair to you. You shouldn't hide your sadness away for the comfort of others. Talk about how you feel as much as you may need to. In fact, the repetition is our brain's way of attempting to make sense of a situation. It's unnatural to talk about a traumatic experience once and never again. If you want to cry for three days straight, go for it. You also don't need to 'be the bigger person' if you don't want to be. In fact, I'll go as far as saying that that type of advice is often weaponised against women. We're encouraged to either not tell our story or to soften the truth of our reality to make past men in our lives feel comfortable. Even my writing this book goes against the grain – because how dare I share my experience unapologetically! Take this as a lesson: you don't have to appear gracious if you don't want to.

So, if post-break-up cortisol is messing with your body, what the hell can you do to practically help yourself? Social support and connections aid to buffer the effects of stress – so seeking help, support or even spending time with family and friends can assist greatly. It's also helpful to be reminded that you're not alone and difficult break-ups have been experienced by most people.

Other things that can help you include mindfulness, meditation and exercise. I know what you're probably thinking: 'Here we go again with all this healthy living bullsh*t.' At least, I assume you're thinking this because that's what I used to think whenever someone tried to push exercise as a remedy for emotional healing. Also, when people would suggest 'mindfulness', I used to think what the hell is 'mindfulness' anyway? I often had images of awkward yoga poses and hippie retreats in my head. But mindfulness is defined in the dictionary as 'a mental state achieved by focusing one's awareness on the present moment, while calmly acknowledging and accepting one's feelings, thoughts, and bodily sensations'. To put it even more simply, mindfulness is about checking in with yourself and self-reflecting in a non-judgmental way. If that's not giving zero accountability, I don't know what is. The goal is to stop being preoccupied with the past or the future and to take in the present, accept things as they are and become deeply aware of your thoughts, feelings and sensations. Something as small as pausing to consider where you're holding your physical tension is a form of mindfulness. Are you currently tensing your shoulders? Do you need to drop them? Are you clenching your jaw as you're reading this sentence? Are your glutes tense or relaxed? Do you need to take five minutes to relax the muscles in your face? Are your brows raised or furrowed? Perhaps you're taking very shallow breaths and you don't even realise you're not breathing properly? Or maybe the tension you hold is in your mind. Are you constantly replaying the past? Do you need to accept your circumstances for what they are? Are you living in a state of self-blame? When done regularly and actively, mindfulness practices have the power to reduce stress, improve emotional control, increase overall life satisfaction and so much more.

Meditation is one popular form of practising mindfulness. Admittedly, I often struggle to 'meditate' in the traditional sense, but I do apply meditation techniques when I pray. Now, I know not everyone is religious, and for that reason, you can adopt this tip however you see fit, but prayer has really helped me through hard times. Even if you're not connected to a higher power, it's comforting to release all your worries and burdens privately. Just through sitting by myself, sharing what I'm going through, letting go of my sadness and asking for spiritual guidance and support makes all the difference to me. If you're someone who isn't particularly spiritual but you want to start mediating, my tips include taking small incremental steps. If your first meditation session is sixty minutes, you'll likely lose focus, get fed up and feel demotivated. Start small. Five-minute sessions at a time is more than enough for centring yourself. As you begin to feel more comfortable, you can begin to make your sessions longer.

It's also important to pick your environment carefully. You want to be in a quiet yet comfortable space. Sitting on your favourite chair or cushion is more than enough. If you want to take it up a notch, sit in a sauna or even get a massage. One of my greatest challenges when I have attempted to meditate has always been trying to remain undistracted. I often feel as if my mind moves at 70mph and for that reason, it tends to wander. My advice to you is to be patient with yourself when this happens. We live such demanding, busy, active lives, so it's unsurprising that the average person may struggle to remain focused on the mental relaxation element of meditation. Give yourself grace when you start thinking about what you're going to order for dinner or your long to-do list of chores. Remind yourself that all those thoughts can wait and don't be hard on yourself for having to refocus.

Since the goal is to meditate with the hope of letting go of post-break-up stress, try to observe your feelings. How are you feeling in the moment? How have you felt throughout the day? Which feelings do you want to let go of? Which feelings do you want to embody? Audit your sadness.

On the topic of exercise, have you ever noticed how, after a break-up, some men like to get in the gym? It's like they turn into bodybuilders overnight. I used to think this was purely a case of acquiring a 'revenge body', but there's some helpful science to suggest that exercise can help people manage the sadness we experience after relationship break-ups. Several studies note how physical activity triggers the release of endorphins, which helps to elevate mood and reduce symptoms of depression and anxiety. Other studies also highlight how exercise can help to regulate our emotional responses, improving mental resilience. In a more obvious way, exercising can also help to improve our overall self-esteem — when we are healthier, we feel better about ourselves. The journey towards building a healthier lifestyle can also be a positive distraction and even provide a sense of community when we undertake it as part of a group or social activity. Put simply, if you're dealing with physical and mental distress, be mindful, get meditating (or praying) and increase your exercise.

On a less scientific level, incorporate personal acts of kindness into your day. Acts of kindness don't have to be extravagant – even just eating your favourite meal, going on a walk, buying yourself flowers or having a self-care day can bring you comfort. Maybe even watching a movie, painting, dancing, reading a book or listening to uplifting music. Whatever it is, doing something that brings you joy is a great way to soothe yourself as you try to process challenging emotions. It's even more of a plus if the thing that brings you comfort is a creative outlet. One thing about creative outlets is that they help us channel our emotions into something tangible, making sadness feel less overwhelming. You think I've always written just for fun? Sometimes, I've written to heal myself.

I also can't disregard the importance of community when it comes to managing sadness. Whether through friends or family, community plays a crucial role in helping people heal. When I've been at my saddest, I've often felt isolated. It's so easy to tell yourself you're all alone when you're navigating painful feelings. The truth is, we're never completely alone. Just hit an online forum and you'll find several variations of your heartbreak story. As disappointing as it is to know hearts are being broken across the globe, it's comforting to know our experience is not uncommon and other people have made it through their own sadness to the other side.

Similar experiences aside, simply spending time in the company of others can provide a nice distraction from sadness. Reminding yourself that you have a support system outside of your ex makes life's challenges feel more manageable. I can't speak for everyone, but in my life, my friends and family do a good job of offering new ways of looking at situations. Being in the company of people who care about me also reminds me of my value. Nobody gasses me up more than my nearest and dearest and a self-esteem boost is so valuable when we may be feeling undervalued. And, of course, social interaction triggers oxytocin, the hormone responsible for building bonds. When one bond is cut, other bonds should be invested in – and in doing so, you will find that your overall well-being will improve.

Some of you may be reading this while feeling

completely alone. What do you do when you don't have loving family or friends? What do you do when your ex-partner was the only social connection in your life? Outside of building new and healthy alternative connections, you can also find community in the form of online or in-person support groups. Community doesn't have to be historical to be meaningful.

With all of this said, the lesson of this chapter is to acknowledge that you're sad if sadness is what you're truly feeling. Do not feel like you must walk on eggshells or hold your tears in to make everyone else around you feel comfortable. Confronting your sadness head-on is a necessary part of healing. Do what you need to do to manage the stress, but in all your endeavours, don't pretend you're feeling okay if you're not.

Shame

You're filled with shame for not having had a 'successful' relationship, and you're also feeling ashamed for 'choosing wrong'. A sense of shame is following you and, in the process, blame has joined in.

The 'shameful woman' is a popular societal archetype. She's the girl who 'stayed too long', who 'should have known better' and who should feel 'ashamed' for her relationship not working out. For whatever reason, when we as women mess up, we get the blame, but when men mess up, we catch strays too. We are often taught to internalise male failure, or break-ups in general, as our own embarrassment to carry.

As I mentioned previously, Mr Dismissive Avoidant and I broke up on more than one occasion. After the first break-up, it was seemingly clear to people who followed us on social media that we were no longer together. Yet, for some reason, I was the only person experiencing online bullying for it. I'd post a picture online and a random woman would write a tweet suggesting I was desperately trying to get him back. I'd share my writing on relationships and I'd see comments from men and women about my inability to 'keep a man' when, in reality, *I* had broken up with *him*. When someone wanted to troll me online, they would always focus on me being single. In hindsight, it's kind of flattering now because they knew they couldn't call me dumb, ugly or unaccomplished. The only thing in my life that they felt they could ridicule was my single status.

I'd be lying if I said that, at the time, it didn't get to me. It did. For a moment, they actually had me feeling a sense of shame for being in a 'failed' relationship as if it failed because of something I did or didn't do? For a second, I started to internalise their trolling and began asking myself whether I was the problem. There's a deeply engrained expectation in society that, as women, we must find a way to blame ourselves under the guise of holding ourselves accountable. We're taught to be good enough, accommodating enough and loving enough – and when a relationship ends, much of the chatter surrounds what we could have done differently. We see this all the time in the celebrity space, particularly with women who have a very public dating history. When their relationships end, the conversation surrounds how they 'can't keep a man', but maybe those men couldn't keep them? Even when it comes to toxic relationships, women are often given little empathy, and instead, they're asked why they didn't leave early enough. 'Ride or die' pop culture teaches women that they must stick around through it all, and that if we don't, we have somehow failed.

While my first break-up with Mr Dismissive Avoidant was ridden with shame, my break-up with Mr What-Was-I-Thinking was filled with shame *and* blame. After my friends told me that he had cheated on me with the girl at the dinner party, I mentally spiralled. It was especially awful because there was no faceless girl involved – I had a face and I had a name, which made me spiral even more. I remember looking the girl up on Facebook (there was no Instagram back then) and thinking 'What exactly did she have that I didn't have? What did she do that I didn't do? Was it my fault?'

For the first time in my life, I was questioning my worth. I remember questioning why Mr What-Was-I-Thinking thought I wasn't enough. I remember asking myself how I may have been able to change the outcome. 'I should have done this, I would have done that, I could have done this.' I asked myself all the questions I now tell other women not to ask themselves – the 'shoulda, woulda, couldas'. I carried a lot of blame, largely because heartbreak, when coupled with betrayal, can be so disorientating. But what I didn't understand back then is that when a man cheats, it is rarely about his partner.

Despite Mr What-Was-I-Thinking cheating on me, he still wanted to remain in a relationship with me. I remember him begging for forgiveness – and I was bewildered. If he wanted to be with me, why the hell did he do what he did? Surely, if a man cheats, it means he's unhappy with the state of his relationship? *Right*?

Wrong. Age and wisdom have taught me that even men in happy relationships are capable of cheating. Some men cheat because they have deep-rooted self-esteem issues that contribute to a desire for validation from anywhere they can receive it, often stemming from either an insecurity or a lack of attention at some point in their lives. Then there are men who simply lack sexual discipline. They have a desire to explore sex with other people out of curiosity, or even a warped fear of missing out. Some lack the impulse control and the self-regulation required to physically commit themselves to one person, and other men cheat for a thrill or excitement. For whatever reason, they're easily bored of stability and they intentionally disrupt the peace in their relationship because chaos makes them feel more at home.

When I took to Facebook after being cheated on to look up 'the other girl', what struck me was that we looked completely different – we had different hair, we were a different shape, we had different features and she was a completely different race to me. I remember thinking, 'Am I not his type? Does he find her prettier? But he pursued me, what changed?' My shoulda, woulda, couldas eventually evolved into me questioning why I wasn't enough. The scandal formed the foundation for a new developing obsession. I suddenly became preoccupied with the other girl in an unhealthy way. I would analyse the few photos she posted of herself online, examining her face, comparing the way she dressed to the way I dressed. I'd even create scenarios in my mind about how they met, how they ended up underneath/on top of each other or hypothetical situations surrounding what I would do if she and I ever crossed paths. My pain and curiosity eventually started fuelling hatred. The sheer image of her face would sicken me, yet at the same time, I couldn't help but search for photos of her. I'd shudder at the echo of her name, yet I'd listen out for updates should anyone mention her. It got to a point where the other girl was on my mind more than Mr What-Was-I-Thinking, despite him being the one who did me dirty – how f*cked up is that?

This is what happens when we hold ourselves accountable for someone else hurting us. We internalise it. We unfortunately see it as a reflection of our value, rather than a reflection of the other person's morals (or more accurately, lack thereof). My obsession regarding the other woman was the result of me viewing Mr What-Was-I-Thinking's cheating as a product of her versus me – when it was really a product of Mr What-Was-I-Thinking versus being a decent human being. What made my distaste for her even more sad was the fact she was actually a victim in all of it too. The story I conjured up in my mind, of her being a villainous witch of a woman who sought to destroy my peace, was far from accurate. She didn't even know I existed in Mr What-Was-I-Thinking's life, and the same way he had lied to me was the same way he had lied to her. In her head, she was the only girl and he had eyes for no one other than her. Coming to this realisation helped me control the negative emotions I was experiencing at the time. It also curbed my 'obsession'. I no longer viewed her as a 'threat' to my self-worth but as someone who could relate to what I was going through. Because, after all, nobody can threaten my self-worth unless I give them permission to. It also reinforced the fact that the real villain of the story was Mr What-Was-I-Thinking.

This reframing helped me deal with my self-blame, but it didn't cure my shame. I still felt very ashamed that I had been cheated on, and even more ashamed that my friends knew about it. But one thing I know now that I wish I knew then is that we're allowed to express shame without taking responsibility for it. Shame and blame don't have to co-exist. You're allowed to express how humiliated and disrespected you feel. You're allowed to acknowledge feelings of embarrassment or the fact you've been mistreated while also acknowledging that none of it was your fault. After I was cheated on, I was mortified! And it's no surprise why. Someone I had put my trust in had not only broken my trust, but their actions were also public knowledge. It was a painful situation to be in.

People often paint the expression of shame as pitiful, but many of us express it not because we desire pity, but because we deserve our truth, and living in truth instead of denial provides healing. If someone has hurt you, hold *them* accountable and express the impact of their hurt with the understanding that the shame you're expressing isn't tied to you being too loyal, being too loving or 'not choosing correctly'. The shame you are carrying is tied to the fact someone else hurt or disrespected you. It's okay for you to express shame in this regard. I'd go as far as even saying that in not acknowledging shame, you give the other person an out. Dismissing the shame is just one way of you cleaning up their mess. The fact is, if a f*ck boy made you feel worthless, let that be your honest account. You don't need to reframe it or soften it to appear noble. As women, we should feel empowered to tell our stories and mention the villains in them if we want to.

I want you to view your shame as a mirror. It's not something you must carry forever – it's something you should hold up as a reflection of the other person. The shame you are feeling is tied to them. It is a reflection of their character and an example of what happens when another person treats their partner carelessly. The shame was not caused by you – it was caused by them. Express it, and in doing so, you will eventually walk away unburdened.

Worry

Worry is one part of heartbreak I was never warned about. After the anger, the sadness and the shame, there's an uncertainty that follows us. It creeps up slowly, like fog under a door, until one day, we feel terrified about the years ahead. 'Will I ever get married? Will I ever have children? Am I running out of time? Is this it for me?' Break-ups don't just remove the person from our life – they remove the plans we once had and the future we thought was secure. And as women, the weight of that stolen future hits harder because we live in a world that is constantly reminding us of our ticking biological clock and all the alleged milestones we are meant to reach by a certain age. It's the type of worry that has had my own friends filled with fear, wondering if they've 'missed their window'. The type of worry that creates a pit in a woman's stomach every time she sees an engagement or pregnancy announcement on social media.

This chapter is for the women who aren't just hurting, they're worrying.

One thing that can push a woman to forgive a no-good man *or* keep a woman in a relationship with a man who isn't meeting her needs is the fear of marrying 'late', or never marrying at all. If you're reading this book as a single woman who is over the age of 25, there's a good chance that you've grappled with this fear at some point. If so, it's unsurprising, as the world has spent so long treating marriage as if it's a necessary part of every woman's life without which she has failed at being a woman.

After Mr Dismissive Avoidant and I broke up, I was often taunted online for being unmarried. In writing about relationships, I, of course, drew attention to myself, but the attention I drew certainly didn't warrant the criticisms I received. At the time, I was in my early thirties, and 'go and marry' seemed to be people's criticism of choice whenever they didn't agree with my opinion. Meanwhile, despite my ex being years older than I am, marriage was never thrown in his face in the same way.

Jane Austen's nineteenth-century novel *Pride and Prejudice* is one of many books that highlights the hold marriage has had on women throughout history:

Mr Collins, to be sure, was neither sensible nor agreeable; his society was irksome, and his attachment to her must be imaginary. But still, he would be her husband. Without thinking highly either of men or matrimony, marriage had always been her object; it was the only provision for well-educated young women of small fortune, and however uncertain of giving happiness, must be their pleasantest preservative from want.

While *Pride and Prejudice* is a work of fiction, it is a work of fiction based on fact. It was written as a reflection of the times and the excerpt above perfectly demonstrates how marriage was viewed by women. Marriage for women in the time of Jane Austen was a matter of necessity. Charlotte Lucas was to marry Mr Collins not because she loved and adored him but because at the 'ripe old age of 27', she feared never marrying – and she needed to marry for provision. As a pragmatic woman of her time, she cast the prospect of love aside and selected Mr Collins for economic security. If you've read the book (or seen the movie), you would know that Mr Collins was a pompous man who had previously unsuccessfully proposed to another woman. Charlotte was not his first choice, but neither of them minded as marriage was a status symbol for them and it was better to marry 'conveniently' than to never marry at all. Their marriage was one that exemplified many marriages of that time, and one might argue that not much has changed today.

More women marry now for love than for economic advancement (thanks to progress surrounding women's rights and our ability to work for our own money), but it can also be said that marriage is still seen as a status symbol in society. I found this to be true after I got engaged. With all the achievements I have acquired in life – from penning books, becoming a bestselling author, having my own podcast and more – I was never as celebrated by people online as I was when a man placed a ring on my finger.

If you're worried about never getting married or marrying 'late', I get it. These aren't silly fears, and you are far from pathetic for worrying about never marrying because, frankly, it's not your fault that you're worrying! The world has made marriage a symbol of success in a woman's life. When men never marry, they are seen as men who choose to not marry, but when women don't marry, we are unfairly viewed as romantic 'failures'. This is insane because there are so many things about marriage that are out of our control, like timing, luck and the mindset of the other person. It's not like writing a book, completing a charity run or executing a strategy because it's not inherently a measure of skill. Unlike achievements that require personal excellence, marriage hinges heavily on mutual compatibility and mutual effort, which doesn't necessarily reflect personal excellence.

I'm not someone who shies away from speaking my mind and not long after my engagement, I made my stance clear. I wrote online that getting married in and of itself is not an achievement. Admittedly, my timing probably wasn't ideal and triggered a few individuals because I got dragged by people all over the world – from Nigeria to London to France. But my opinion hasn't changed. It's actually very easy to just 'get married'. Somewhere in the world is a man searching for a foreign wife because he's desperate for a visa. While I'm typing this, someone visiting Vegas got married today 'just because'. Did you know that in some parts of the world, you can even marry individuals who are currently incarcerated? As long as people are desperate for marriage – even if it's for an ulterior motive – there will always be someone available to marry. To add, some marriages are just terrible. They were terrible at the start, terrible during and will always be terrible. Is it an achievement to be married to someone toxic whom you may even detest? Marriage on its own is no achievement. Some may argue that the achievement lies in having a long-lasting marriage, but long-lasting doesn't automatically equal 'good'. Many of us know at least one miserable older couple – whether it's your uncle and aunt, grandparents or even your parents – who remain together for the sake of reputational preservation or a sense of 'duty' over a sense of love. Marrying someone you adore who treats you well is certainly a blessing, but the achievement is in personal fulfilment.

I walked down the aisle at age 36 – an 'old bride' by nineteenth-century standards, at the time of Jane Austen, and an older-than-average bride by today's standards (the average age of a first-time bride in the UK and US ranges from 29 to 31). In my twenties, when I was with Mr Dismissive Avoidant, marriage was something I wanted because I had a limited sense of identity. I wanted to tick a box, and I thought ticking that box would add fulfilment to my life. If you've just gone through a break-up that has left you worried about getting married, I want to tell you that marrying for marriage's sake is one of the biggest mistakes any woman can make because marrying the wrong person can have such a detrimental impact on the quality and length of your existence.

According to Paul Dolan, Professor of Behavioural Science at the London School of Economics, single childless women are the happiest in society. Why? Because the benefits derived from marriage for men are not the same as for women. For one, numerous studies have found that married men tend to earn more at work than their unmarried counterparts – a phenomenon known as the 'male marriage wage premium'. In addition, several studies indicate that married men boast a higher life expectancy than single men and better health outcomes, including lower rates of heart disease, a lower risk of depression, reduced blood pressure, a lower risk of stroke, better recovery rates and more. At this point, you can probably guess that the same isn't true for women. For women, it's quite the opposite.

Plenty of research suggests that married women typically earn less than single women. Unlike married men who experience a 'male marriage wage premium', many married women face a 'motherhood penalty'. Married women, particularly women who have children, often experience salary reductions. This could be down to employer bias (with some employers believing married women are less committed to their careers) or reduced working hours due to responsibilities tied to household labour and childcare. In addition, a 2006 Journal of Population Economics study titled 'The gender longevity gap' found that, on average, married women had a shorter life expectancy than their single counterparts. Studies also suggest that healthcare outcomes are worse for married women, with married women reporting more psychological issues than single women and higher dementia rates.

For women, being married can come with a range of negative implications, whether it's increased stress and anxiety, emotional pressure, increased levels of unpaid domestic labour, slower professional advancement, a loss of autonomy, financial dependence or more. At this point, you're probably thinking, 'If marriage is really so bad, why the hell did you get married?' Well, I think many of these negative implications are tied to marrying the wrong type of person. Whether it's increased stress from an unfair division of household labour, anxiety from being disrespected, increased emotional pressure from being undervalued or a loss of autonomy from being with a controlling partner. With a caring and loving partner, marriage can provide companionship, emotional and physical support, financial security and shared physical and legal responsibility for raising children. But with all the potential negative implications tied to marriage, marrying for marriage's sake is just not worth it.

My husband is a beautiful man, and when I use this adjective, I'm not referring to his appearance (although he's beautiful to look at too). He is one of the most gentle, considerate men that I know. Since he entered my life, my life has been easier, happier and more rewarding. He has a knack for making the challenges I face appear less daunting and he adds to my joy, bringing comfort and laughter to those around him. Based on what he says, I do the same for him. However, had I not met a man as kind and as loving as my husband, I wouldn't have chosen marriage. I craved it for a sense of purpose in my early twenties, but after the breakdown of my relationship with Mr Dismissive Avoidant and the growth that came with that, I concluded that getting married just to say I did it was a torturous act and would actually bring little benefit to my life bar people being able to say, 'Well at least you're married.' I chose to get married in my mid-thirties because I married a man who adds value, and should he cease to add value, then I will cease to be married – likewise, should I cease to add value to his life, he will do what is best for his own wellbeing. The goal for us isn't simply just 'being married'; it's about constantly providing mutual value to one another.

When you get to a place of living for personal fulfilment instead of the validation of outsiders, you stop viewing marriage as a necessary milestone. Is companionship a wonderful thing? Of course, but companionship is not limited to the confines of marriage. Marriage, of course, comes with legal implications that can be beneficial under the right circumstances, but companionship comes in many forms. I'm not saying it's wrong to desire marriage – many women do. Just ask yourself why. It's important that whatever decision you make, it's done with your wellbeing in mind. Do you want to get married to satisfy other people or is it because you desire the permanency that comes with this type of companionship?

If you are sure that marriage is something you desire, I want to stress that it is better to marry well than to marry early. Don't let the post-break-up worry you're feeling pressure you into simply selecting any man who is open to marriage. Marriage is far too significant of a commitment to undertake it with just anybody.

With that said, I know that many of my friends who have worried about not getting married were less pressed about the marriage and more fearful about the time they had left to have children. If it's not marriage worries – it's motherhood worries.

Now, I'm not going to disregard science and the fact that women see a gradual decline in their fertility in their late twenties – but what I want to do is stress how gradual that decline truly is. For a long time, I was under the impression that from 30, having a child is tough, and from 35, it's almost mythical, but that just isn't the case. Studies have shown that by age 35, approximately 65% of women will conceive within one year and roughly 84% will conceive within four years. When we're told that by 35 women's fertility drops by half, what people fail to mention is that the half in question goes from a 20% chance of pregnancy per month in your mid-twenties to a 10% chance of pregnancy per month in your mid-thirties. When I was younger, all the fertility fearmongering led me to assume that our rate of pregnancy went from say 90% in our twenties to 10% in our thirties, but the actual drop isn't that huge at all. In fact, studies suggest that by age 40, approximately 44% of women who are trying to get pregnant will conceive within a year. To add, women are not the only people who experience biological changes linked to fertility as they age. Many studies highlight a noticeable decline in sperm quality for men from around the age of 35. As a man ages, his sperm count reduces, gets gradually less mobile and increases in abnormalities – yet men are rarely pressured to procreate like we are.

Women worry after break-ups because society has told us there is a biological deadline. So, if a break-up in your late twenties or thirties has you stressing about motherhood, please take it easy. You still have time. And if you're not sure, maybe put yourself at ease and get a fertility test done. I took a test and learned things about my fertility that helped me make more informed choices about my relationships and my personal timelines.

Also, be mindful that the world is changing. More women are having children in their thirties and forties than ever before. More women have a better understanding of the sheer gravity of work involved in raising a child and, for that reason, they (including myself) focus more on building a solid foundation for their kids before introducing them into this world.

Whatever you choose to do regarding getting married or becoming a parent, just do it for the right reasons. And in all that you do, prioritise quality over getting things done quickly out of worry.

Loneliness

Your bed feels a little colder, and your phone rarely goes off anymore. Suddenly, you're feeling something you haven't experienced in a while . . . and that's loneliness.

Loneliness after a break-up is a common response to a broken heart, particularly if you and your partner spent a lot of time together. You go from saying good morning and goodnight to the same person for months or even years to suddenly saying absolutely nothing at all. You go from running to share your good news with one person to feeling like your celebrations just aren't hitting in the same way. You go from planning a present and a future with one person to feeling like you must start all over again. One of the immediate challenges *women* typically face after a break-up is feeling lonely. I wanted to specify 'women' because multiple studies indicate that women experience higher levels of immediate post-break-up loneliness when compared with men.

Before we get into the meat of this chapter, I want to explore this phenomenon a little more. Why might this be the case? Why does loneliness have an immediate impact on women? First off, research suggests that women tend to process and reflect on the impact of break-ups more quickly than men (who tend to suppress their emotions). This processing and reflecting can lead to a range of other emotions which contribute to feeling lonely. In general, women also release higher levels of oxytocin (the bonding hormone) during relationships. When a relationship ends, the sudden drop in oxytocin can lead to rapid low mood, which can slowly manifest as loneliness. The nature of heterosexual relationships in society also typically sees women adjust their lives and routines to accommodate partners, so when a relationship ends, it can lead to a sudden change in routine that some women might find rather disruptive or unsettling.

If your heartbreak was recent and you feel particularly lonely, there's a reason for it. Your mind and body are simply trying to process what happened and adjust to change. Loneliness is a painful emotion, but also one that is quite taboo to express – because in a world that screams 'love yourself', you may even feel guilty for feeling lonely, but that can happen in the absence of companionship. In this moment, you may even be feeling frustrated at the thought of your ex seemingly living life without a care in the world, but things aren't always what they seem. In fact, research suggests that, over time, men eventually report higher levels of loneliness overall. It just isn't initially obvious because it's delayed. That flirty feeling of freedom men display immediately after a break-up often hits them like a ton of bricks weeks or months later, which may explain the common 'Hey stranger' text women tend to receive months after they've parted ways with a guy. The fact is, when you suppress your loneliness, it only hits harder in the future, so I want you to acknowledge yours – and reframe it.

One thing that helped me manage my own feelings of loneliness was defining loneliness and solitude as two different things. The dictionary definition of solitude is the state or situation of being alone. Sometimes, we exist in a state of solitude out of choice and other times, it's a result of circumstance, but solitude is a state of being, not a state of feeling. Loneliness, however, is defined as 'sadness because one has no friends or company'. Loneliness is not simply a state of being but also one of feeling, and one thing I love about feelings is the degree of control we have over them.

I can certify that loneliness is a state of feeling and not 'being' because in my loneliest moments I was rarely alone. In my loneliest moments, I was simply in the presence of people who didn't truly understand me or value me. I was in the presence of people who focused more on what they could take from me than give to me. I was in the presence of people who treated me like I was an accessory or an extra in their story. In fact, I've felt lonelier in certain past relationships than I've ever felt as a single woman – and that's telling. If you're newly single, you may be frightened at the thought of remaining 'lonely' but I'm here to tell you that this window of singleness doesn't have to be a lonely period. Singleness is also not a punishment, nor is it a pit stop you should resent. It's an opportunity for you to focus solely on yourself and pour into yourself entirely. It's also much better to be single and at peace than in a relationship with someone who isn't pouring into you and doesn't value you.

To redefine loneliness as solitude, you first need to name the feeling without judgment. Loneliness can often feel like something vital is missing, so instead of saying 'I'm lonely', acknowledge that you are living life as you once lived it in the past – as an independent person, and it only feels unfamiliar because you haven't done it for a while. You might be 'alone', but you've been alone before and life didn't feel so bleak. In your solitude, consider how you can take stock of the things in your life that you may have forgotten about.

In the aftermath of a break-up, one of the best things you can do for yourself in your time of solitude is to turn your selfish dial up. For some people, selfishness looks like cruelty, but for a woman who has been hurt by a man, selfishness is clarity. It's not about being spiteful or revengeful; it's about no longer living your life according to people's expectations of you. It's about no longer living to make other people comfortable. It's about focusing less on satisfying others and instead on satisfying yourself.

Initially, this concept may make you squirm a little. After all, society is still uncomfortable with women who choose themselves. We live in a patriarchal world, developed by men and made for men. It's a system that prioritises men's desires and enforces gender inequality. It contributes to men believing they should get what they want and chase their dreams at all costs; meanwhile women are encouraged to be submissive followers of men who put their own desires on the back burner. We are taught to be accommodating, so to consider becoming a selfish woman in a patriarchal world is a total act of rebellion.

So, why do it? Well, in my opinion, a woman who embraces selfishness during solitude goes through a transformational process. It's the moment when a woman, shattered by betrayal or hurt, stops being of service to others. It's a moment where she rejects social norms for the betterment of her mental and physical health. It's a rebirth for her, a restorative window of time where she realises how much she has poured into people who barely poured into her. It's a moment where she suddenly sees how much of her life was shaped by societal pressures and obligation instead of her personal desires. The moment a woman chooses to be selfish after a break-up, she makes the decision to no longer abandon herself for others. She chooses herself.

So, how do you do it? Well, the first step to being more selfish during this time is to be honest about what you want to get out of your life – without apologising for it. Also, be honest about how you feel without pussyfooting around when people ask about why you and your ex broke up. Know that you don't have to be the bigger person. You can be fully expressive without needing to consider other people's feelings. Free yourself of the constraints tied to women performing their pain to make other people comfortable. If you don't want to speak to your ex's friends and family anymore, then don't. You also don't owe anyone an explanation, and you don't have to entertain reconciliation with your ex to make anyone feel better. When you're selfish, you can stop performing and take on an 'it is what it is' attitude. In becoming more selfish, you'll also become stricter with your boundaries. If you don't want to do something, you simply don't do it. Don't feel guilty for enforcing boundaries you were once open to negotiating. No matter what people suggest, you're allowed to change your mind about things. Know that now is the time to start making decisions purely for yourself – because you are no longer burdened by being accountable to someone else. The beauty of the solitude you have is that you can do what you want, when you want, on your own terms – whether it's moving to a new city, starting a new job, or totally reinventing yourself. If indulgence is what you want, satisfy that feeling. Book that flight, spoil yourself, prioritise your needs more than you have ever done before. The world is your oyster. What do you enjoy doing? If when you were with your ex, you stopped doing anything that you love, now is the time to start again. Reconnect with your passions. Even if you didn't stop, it's time to reignite your interests. Use this time of solitude to recreate a version of yourself that centres your own joy before anybody else's. What does your dream life look like? Think about how you can upgrade your life with your happiness at the centre – because you no longer have to consider anyone else's happiness but your own. Set new and higher standards that you are comfortable with. Ask yourself what kind of life you want so you can start taking the steps to build it.

Now for the extra fun part. Imagine that you are your dream woman already. Imagine you have acquired your dream life. What actions do you think you took to get there? Get practical and intentional about the changes you need to make.

The breakdown of my relationship with Mr Dismissive Avoidant ended up being one of the best things that has ever happened to me because it triggered a series of events that eventually kickstarted my career and shaped my sense of identity. I lost one thing, but in losing that thing, I found myself. The selfishness I incorporated into my life led me to invest in myself in ways I had never done before. I networked, I explored the world, I shared my thoughts in my writing with a total disregard for how it might rub people the wrong way – and that changed my life for the better. I wrote a bestselling book, I stopped silencing myself, I became more audacious (because I felt like I really had nothing to lose at that point) and I also made myself the main character. Before the break-up, my adult life was very much about him and 'us', but after the break-up, it became all about me.

Interestingly, I'm not alone when it comes to heartbreak kickstarting one of the best parts of my life. A 2013 Kingston University study by Andrew E. Clark and Yannis Georgellis surveyed 10,000 individuals between the ages of 16 and 60 over twenty years and asked these participants to evaluate their happiness levels before and after significant life events. The study found that most women experienced a significant increase in happiness and contentment following a divorce, lasting up to five years after their marriage concluded. This elevation in happiness even surpassed their typical or average life satisfaction levels. Outside of this survey, there are many anecdotal reports available to us from women who say their lives improved after a break-up. I think it's safe to assume that the majority of these women likely didn't take the breakdown of their relationship well and might have struggled immediately afterwards. We can also safely infer that many of them assumed their life would probably go downhill after their relationship ended. But this isn't the case for lots of women. Things typically improve after break-ups because we learn to prioritise ourselves more.

Being overly considerate in any sort of social dynamic isn't healthy. You end up people-pleasing, avoiding conflict, disregarding your desires and dismissing your boundaries. That's a big reason why I wanted this guide to focus so heavily on *not* holding yourself accountable. Women can be too thoughtful – always questioning how they have impacted others and how they can help others while never considering the reverse. I once saw a clip online of actress Viola Davis that echoed this sentiment. In her words, 'When it comes down to disappointing other people or disappointing yourself, choose other people all the time. In fact, it is your job in life to disappoint as many people as you can so that you do not disappoint yourself.' For your own fulfilment, you need to stop considering everyone else all the time and start considering yourself.

In my first book, I mentioned that 'not all losses are losses'. In the moment, heartbreak is devastating. Losing a lover is one of the most difficult losses to navigate, outside of dealing with a bereavement or a friendship break-up.

But eventually you will prosper because heartbreak grants you the opportunity to be self-focused. With no partner around, it means *you* can be that little bit more selfish.

I once held a live Q&A on one of my social media platforms and someone asked me what I miss most about being single. The answer was easy for me: I missed being completely selfish. I missed doing exactly what I wanted to do without considering the needs of another person. I missed not having to manage another person's expectations or preferences. I missed not having to explain any of my choices or decisions. I could prioritise myself with zero guilt when I was single and, subsequently, even more of my energy could go into self-improvement. Sometimes, I even miss the solitude! As much as I adore my husband, and as much as I prioritise my wellbeing, being in a relationship requires a willingness to compromise on occasion and consider someone else. Even when the relationship is good, the positive feelings can consume you and if you're not disciplined, those positive thoughts and emotions can distract you from other important priorities. There have been days in my life that I could have invested in work but instead, I invested them in spending time with a romantic partner. My time also has to be shared. However, when I was single, I was focused solely on my own wants and my own personal growth and that selfish period contributed to many personal wins. This may be why it's not uncommon to see women elevate to greater heights after leaving relationships that weren't serving them, whether it's Rihanna growing from a musician to a multi-talented billionaire businesswoman after her break-up from Chris Brown, Nicole Kidman winning an Academy Award after her divorce from Tom Cruise, Tina Turner becoming a musical icon after leaving Ike Turner or Elizabeth Taylor coming back stronger after each of her seven divorces. Some might say that when a relationship wasn't good for us and it ends, the universe has a way of letting us know that was the best outcome.

As painful as loneliness might immediately feel, when we reframe it, it can make room for a transformative process in our life. That period of rediscovering who you are, when you are accountable to nobody but yourself, is a period of time that you shouldn't take for granted. Redefining loneliness, and yourself in the process, will bless you with some of the most amazing memories and opportunities of your life.

Nostalgia

It's been weeks, maybe even months, and he's finally gotten back in touch. How do I know this? Because nine times out of ten, they always do. Especially when they know you're pouring into yourself and levelling up. You try to act unbothered when discussing it with friends but deep down you're pleased. Maybe even ecstatic. But what does it all mean? Has he come to his senses? Does he finally want to act right? Does this mean you're the one who got away? After going through a break-up, we can easily glamorise the memory of our exes.

PARK ALL THOSE THOUGHTS RIGHT NOW.

That's nostalgia. Nostalgia is a powerful emotion made up of a pinch of memory, lots of longing and a spoonful of fantasy. Nostalgia rarely paints an honest picture of the past. Instead, it rounds up the highlights, remixes the hard parts and paints a more beautiful rendition of what truly occurred. When it comes to this topic, I'm an expert. Largely because I've been through this experience too many times to count.

I shared earlier that Mr Dismissive Avoidant and I took several breaks and made up more times than I can count. One contributing factor was the nostalgia I'd feel after the initial hurt had subsided. I'd scroll through videos and photos of the 'good times', I'd ruminate on the lovely memories we shared. I'd read old texts over and the words of affirmation would echo in my mind as if he had shared them in the present moment. At one point, I'd even compare new people to him, forgetting how difficult our relationship was in real time. Nostalgia turned my memory of him into a Hollywood block-buster, so when he would eventually hit me with that 'I miss you' text weeks later, it would work like a charm. Little did I realise at the time, this behaviour enabled me to do everything but move on. I'd cling on to that nostalgia and overexaggerate the positive impact he had in my life and it was that emotion that would keep me emotionally sucked in.

Nostalgia can truly make a bad or mediocre thing seem much more impressive, and before you know it, your brain begins developing feelings of loneliness by exaggerating how good it was. 'Maybe he wasn't so bad after all? Maybe he's as good as it gets? Maybe I was asking for too much? Maybe I'll never do better?' It's a feeling most women have grappled with at some point, including many of my friends.

An old friend of mine once met a guy on vacation. It was 'lust' at first sight. Both her and the guy were immediately drawn to one another and what started off as a holiday romance turned into a long-distance love. They would speak on the phone daily and he would occasionally fly her out to his country of residence so they could spend quality time together. Initially, he seemed perfect because he was just her type – tall, bearded, ambitious, charismatic, intelligent – he appeared to have it all. That is until his emotional unavailability eventually crept to the surface. After just a few months, she noticed a range of behaviours in him that she couldn't stand, and he quickly shapeshifted from Mr Ideal to Mr No-Can-Do. In the end, they went their separate ways, but considering they only dated for about six months in total, it took her a while to get over him.

Now, don't get me wrong, her life wasn't on standstill. She still made the effort to get to know other guys, and even dated a couple for a while, but in the back of her mind was always Mr No-Can-Do. She was haunted by lingering thoughts of what could have been and whether she had made the right choice about calling it quits. Much of her thoughts centred around how much of 'a catch' he was on paper (the looks, the success, the charm). It was as if she eventually convinced herself that he was the one who got away, despite the fact she was the one who left.

After having numerous conversations about Mr No-Can-Do and spending the best part of two years attempting to provide helpful advice to my friend, I suddenly had an 'aha moment'. There was a reason she couldn't let the thought of him shift. There was a reason why she had romanticised the thought of him to the point that she couldn't let go of their separation. It wasn't that he was this incredibly loving, considerate, kind man (because he lacked in all those areas). It was because, to her, he was the best so far. Of all the men she had ever dated, he was the best of them. So, in her mind, she had lost her 'very best', despite him not being good enough.

He was the best to her simply because he was the best of a bad bunch. Unfortunately, she hadn't had the best of luck when it came to love, as she was often drawn to men who lacked emotional availability. Now as for Mr No-Can-Do, he was miles above all the others when it came to his career, his intelligence, his financial status and his charisma, but the fact remained that he was still emotionally unavailable like all the men who came before him. He was just packaged a little better. This premium packaging, however, had her nostalgia on overdrive. Her memories of him seemed much more amazing than they were because she didn't have many great memories of anyone else. Sometimes, we can find ourselves feeling nostalgic over a guy, not because he is great but because everyone we previously dated was terrible.

In my own state of nostalgia, Mr Dismissive Avoidant and I found ourselves in a constant push and pull cycle. We would take a break, then he would resurface and I would pull him in, praying he had gone through some transformational experience or had done some life-altering inner work that brought him clarity about how amazing I truly was as a partner. But hilariously, each time I let nostalgia win, I'd be quickly reminded why I shouldn't have.

It's somewhat frustrating and amusing what we tell ourselves when our emotions take over our logical brain. The same way my anxiety can sometimes lead me to assume the worst after certain interactions is the same way nostalgia and my love for Mr Dismissive Avoidant led me to assume things meant way more than they did. When you feed your nostalgia, your longing can create a storyline built around what you want, not what is truly taking place. The memories you have will then skew, because what you truly want is to stop hurting and filling a pained brain with rose-tinted memories is one way we try to deceive ourselves into feeling better.

Once upon a time, I remember a friend lamenting to me in my twenties about how she missed her ex. The man was terrible to her. In my mind, there was nothing to miss, and with me being me, I was vocal about that. She ended up explaining that she didn't actually miss *him*, but she missed the sex. In her words, 'there's just something about toxic men' that makes them great in bed. The thing is, this isn't an uncommon thought process among young women. I've read similar things online. For many women, the best sex they claim to have ever had was with a f*ck boy, and I think I may be able to explain why. I personally don't believe toxic men are better in bed by default. I think that when we are starved of real love and none of our emotional needs are met, we can end up overvaluing sex as it's the only form of intimacy we are receiving. Have you ever been on a fast before? Whether it's a health fast or spiritual fast, one thing all fasts have in common is how satisfying the first sip of water or bite of food is. A basic meal can taste amazing after a fast because of how deprived of sustenance you've been. That's how I view toxic d*ck. When you're being starved of emotional intimacy, that little crumb of mediocre D can feel amazing. Now, that's not to say every toxic man is actually bad in bed, I'm sure some may be more than satisfactory. But for the most part, it's very easy to grossly exaggerate sexual experiences with men who feed none of our emotional needs. It's also easy to grossly exaggerate the physical intimacy we once shared with someone when we're not experiencing any physical intimacy at all. Nostalgia can have you thinking okay sex was great sex – just because you miss sex! Consider this perspective next time you feel yourself ruminating over a man with poor character. Was he actually good? Or is nostalgia tricking you into thinking he was?

In the past, each time any of my exes returned, I told

myself it was because they loved me so deeply and finally wanted to 'act right'. I told myself that I was just so amazing that they couldn't get enough. The thing is, I was and still am amazing. They did in fact know this. But what they also knew is that while I was amazing to them, they didn't have to be that amazing to me. They knew how powerful my nostalgia was and that eventually, I would grant them access and they could experience all the amazing benefits of being attached to me without administering any real change. In hindsight, the thing they *really* missed was my willingness and capacity to love. They missed me pouring into them. They never returned because they were ready to pour into me.

Beyond nostalgia, another reason why we may let exes back in is a desire for closure. According to the Cambridge Dictionary, closure is 'the feeling or act of bringing an unpleasant situation, time, or experience to an end, so that you are able to start new activities'. While I understand that closure can be helpful for people in certain situations, I'm no longer someone who pushes for closure after the end of a relationship. The whole 'so you are able to start new activities' side of closure honestly rubs me the wrong way because why can't I start new activities without these answers?! And this is where zero accountability comes in. Why must I get an answer from anyone to restart my life? When you adopt a zero-accountability mindset, you realise that you don't need a satisfying ending or a meaningful explanation to walk away from something that's already broken. You understand that closure places power into the hands of the other person. If I seek closure from someone, I give them more control – and personally, I don't like that because my life is mine to control. You don't need to meet that man or speak to him for closure. Also, if you currently desire closure, ask yourself where this desire is stemming from. Are you clinging on to 'hope', secretly wishing to reconcile with him? Sometimes what we label 'a desire for closure' is a desire to remain emotionally invested in an ex. But the thing is, you don't need any further clarity. You owe yourself the freedom to move on, not explanations. The longer you search for answers and put your healing in his hands, then the longer you delay your healing. But men know this, and that's often why they never want you to cut the cord entirely . . .

'I'd really like it if we could remain friends.' I remember hearing this from Mr Dismissive Avoidant after our final break-up. Friends? I dabbled with the thought initially. After all, this was someone I loved who told me he loved me in return, but for various reasons, we just weren't working, and maybe remaining friends was the gateway to making us work? The thing is, I had tried that with him before. We would be friends then he would attempt to cross over the friend boundary to the relationship boundary – whether this was through sex, romantic gestures or intimate conversation. Then, in my confusion, I'd ask what was going on, and I'd be hit with, 'But you know what's going on, I said I want to be friends.' The audacity. The gall. I had to learn the hard way – f*ck being friends.

It's important you understand that some men want to maintain a 'friendship' with you to retain access to you. It has nothing to do with genuinely wanting to be there for you in the same way your other friends are there for you. They just want to keep you in their life while maintaining their single status. That way, they can have their single 'fun' without penalty and you will still be on the sidelines to provide emotional support. They are also often very aware that their ongoing presence in your life will make it a little bit more challenging for you to move on. After all, how many guys are really trying to date a woman who's friends with an ex? And how easy is it to truly move on when your ex is lingering in the background? When a relationship ends because the guy wasn't acting right and then he asks to maintain a friendship afterwards, I personally believe that in most cases it's a manipulation tactic that rarely benefits the woman. When it comes to being friends with an ex, the question I'd ask my own girlfriends in the same dilemma is 'What do you gain from being friends with him?' Sure, some exes remain genuine friends, but those are typically relationships that didn't end as a result of debilitating heartbreak or disrespect.

I was once asked by one of my social media followers why it takes people losing us for them to finally see our value. 'Why is it that men fight so hard for our love only when we're no longer part of their life?' After Mr Dismissive Avoidant and I finally parted ways for the last time, he blocked me on everything. Instagram, TikTok, Twitter – you name it. Yet, the push and pull cycle we birthed proved itself to be ongoing, because many years later, I eventually heard from him – via email no less.

Now, the younger me would have been so flattered, thinking, 'Wow, he blocked me on everything and still found a way to get in touch. He must really love me.'

But the me of my thirties wasn't surprised. After all, I was flourishing. My career was at an all-time high, I was looking the best I've ever looked and I was in the happiest relationship of my life – one that had me shouting from the rooftops. I saw the email and sighed a deep sigh, with the understanding that it wasn't something to be flattered about.

The thing is, when men finally lose access to us and fight for their way back in, it can *appear* as if they have suddenly learned to value us. Our nostalgia encourages us to paint a beautiful picture of a painful truth. The truth is that in most cases, the 'worth' they now see is typically tied to what they want us to keep doing for them – not what they are willing to do for us. Or, they have seen how in applying selfishness, we have flourished without them and they can't bear to miss out on the evolved version of us. Then there are the exes who return because the only thing they desire from us is an ego boost. They have something to prove to themselves, not us. They want to see if we'll make space and time for them. They want to know whether we'll give them access. Why? Because granting them access after they've contributed to the breakdown of the relationship tells them that we value their company more than we value our own peace or non-negotiables. It tells them that we still seek their validation. It tells them that we're willing to disregard our boundaries for a chance to reconnect with them. If we are with someone new, it tells them we value reconnecting with them over the feelings of our new partner. It gives them a boost of confidence that many men desperately seek. This type of confidence boost relies on taking advantage of our loneliness or our nostalgia. They want to know that they've 'still got it' and they want to know we'll 'still have it'. But that man doesn't want to be your friend. That man isn't going to return with a new perspective and a new willingness to pour into you. Nor is 'closure' necessary. Men love returning if they think they'll be heard, so be sure to secure the perimeter of your heart. Don't build a picket fence. Build a reinforced steel wall.

What does this wall look like? Block him on every social media app you use. Block his number. Block his email address. Stop checking in with his friends and family under the guise of care when all you really want is a subtle update. Don't make that burner account so you can lurk on his page in disguise. Already made the account? Delete it. Nobody has to know. If he manages to intercept you in person, give him your best unbothered smile and tell him you'd prefer to not talk. One thing about men: they have audacity and will always try their luck. You have to remember that whatever broke you up hasn't suddenly become irrelevant. Don't let nostalgia win. Don't reconnect with him. If you want to truly move on with haste, attempt to kill any fragment of nostalgia you may have.

Once upon a time, I came up with a range of questions to help me (and other women) kill their nostalgia and determine whether someone was worth staying with. I initially shared these questions in an online video titled 'Questions you should ask yourself before marrying that man' and it went viral in just 24 hours. If you're still feeling nostalgic about an ex, here are a few questions which may just help you find clarity and stop romanticising your memory of him:

If you had a son who was just like him, would you be proud of him? Is he a kind man, an honest man, a man of integrity? Would you be proud of the job you have done as a mother if he was your son?
I think this question is important because when we are in love with a man, we can often view him from one lens – the lover lens. In considering his character

and changing him from your partner to your potential future son, you're able to analyse his flaws and strengths in a different way. For example, you might put up with his inconsistent communication and regular omissions as his partner because you have a soft spot for him, but would you want a son who rarely stayed in touch or constantly withheld import-ant information from you? Alternatively, what if you had a daughter and that was her partner? Would you feel like that's the best type of partner for her? If not, why would you tolerate things that you wouldn't want your own child to tolerate?

If he did not change at all, would you still want him? Would you still want him if he remained exactly as he is now, forever?

This question is one that should encourage you to reflect on whether you are in love with the man you know or the potential of the man you know. One thing we are unfortunately great at doing is falling for poten-tial. We can unknowingly find ourselves in relationships with men, not for who they are but who we want them to be and who we think they can evolve into. The sad truth is not everyone evolves. The potential you see in a man may never actually manifest, so the question you must ask yourself is 'If he stayed the same, would I still want him?'

If the two of you had a family and, God forbid, something happened to you, would you trust him to raise your kids well and to be active and present?

This is a very pertinent question if you want to have children at some point in the future, or if you already have kids. Do you believe that the man you're pining over is capable of raising kids without you? If the answer is no, then you may as well be a single parent because you're basically asserting that he will rely on you to do almost everything when it comes to parenting – and that is definitely not the type of man a woman should be marrying if she values her wellbeing.

Think of his worst traits. If his worst traits doubled or even tripled in severity, would you still want him?

Like all men, my husband is not perfect. He, like I, has flaws. But even if his worst traits were exaggerated, I would still choose him because his worst traits don't align with any of my non-negotiables. He does little annoying things but nothing I'd crash out over. If the thought of doubling or tripling your ex's worst traits makes you shudder, why tolerate the single worst trait now?

If answering those questions hasn't silenced your nostalgia, I don't know what will. Please feel free to return to these questions any time you start daydreaming about the person who broke your heart. When you allow nostalgia to be louder than reality, you only delay your healing. That is, unless it's nostalgia about your own life.

There are two types of post-heartbreak nostalgia. There's the destructive nostalgia that rewrites history and keeps us tethered to a warped version of reality, and then there's the productive type that reminds us of what we once loved about ourselves and our life before we met our ex. I want you to be nostalgic, but not about your past relationship. I want you to scroll through old photos and videos, but of the girls trip you took in 2021. I want you to play old songs, but the type that had you hyped to go on a night out before you met *him*. I want you to romanticise your single life, and if you want to feel nostalgic, daydream about the years before your ex.

Hope

Nostalgia encourages us to review the past, but eventually, we have to start considering the future, and that's when hope comes into play. There's a type of hope you *need*. It's the type of hope you have for yourself, about your own life – beyond a romantic partner.

I think it's fair to assume that you're currently in a place where you may have lost a little hope when it comes to love. This is normal. Heartbreak can have you doubting all types of things, including yourself, your future and whether decent men even exist. Admittedly, there are plenty terrible men in this world, but one thing

I want you to know is that good men do certainly exist – and your ex is not at the top of the hierarchy.

In the aftermath of a break-up, it's easy to internalise rejection, but I want you to cling on to hope when it comes to your own outcomes. Because it's that hope that will have you daydreaming again, living again and looking forward to what's ahead. In being hopeful, you can remind yourself that you are not defined by your break-up and that you won't feel sad forever. Hope can be such an asset in our healing journey because in being hopeful, we are reminded that pain isn't permanent. Hope encourages us to cling on to the reality that there will be happier days ahead and it gives us a reason to keep going even when our heart feels heavy. Hope is also important for helping us rebuild our self-worth because it shifts our focus from the break-up we experienced to the possibilities ahead of us. And in being excited about future possibilities, hope encourages us to invest in ourselves again. It opens the doors to new beginnings.

After Mr Dismissive Avoidant and I broke up, I remained hopeful about the future because my prior break-up showed me things get better. While my relationship with Mr Dismissive Avoidant wasn't perfect, it was certainly less turbulent and less hurtful than my relationship with Mr What-Was-I-Thinking, and I was hopeful that there was even better out there for me. Life showed me that I was right. I went from a terrible relationship in university, to a mediocre relationship in my mid-twenties, to a good relationship at 31 and a great relationship at 33. I'm now 36 and married to the man I had the great relationship with. Every relationship got better and I maintained a positive perspective despite previous relationships not working out. Each break-up I experienced also birthed an opportunity for me to pour into myself. In losing him, I gained my time to be selfish, which fed my hopefulness. Break-ups don't just mark an ending – they create space for things you forgot you wanted and, eventually, for someone who chooses you and loves you in the way you deserve. Please believe that you will find another partner, one even better than the one you are currently grieving. There will always be someone kinder than your ex, more attractive than your ex, funnier than your ex and so on and so forth. The world is full of men to choose from. They may not all be great, but there is definitely someone greater than the man who broke your heart, and thinking otherwise is just another way you limit yourself.

I have an abundance mindset, thanks to having an

abundance-mindset mother who instilled it in me. Regardless of how questionable certain men have behaved in my life, I was always under the impression that they were never the pinnacle. If you don't have an abundance-mindset mother, let me be your abundance-mindset sister. There is so much available to you in this world as long as you believe there is! If you do ever feel as if a man is the best you will ever get, I'm not going to hold you accountable. You have zero accountability – because chances are, he manipulated you into believing he was.

One pathetic thing some men like to do is encourage women to believe that settling is a must. There are certain men who revel in suggesting that women can't do any better than the bare minimum, and they live to kill a woman's hope. I have experienced this myself, particularly as a woman who is highly visible online and unashamedly opinionated. Men have told me that nobody would want me due to my age. They've told me I ask for too much. They've told me my relationship expectations are unrealistic. They've told me I will be alone forever because no man wants to partner with an opinionated woman. The funny thing is, all those projections have been proven false, and I'm proud of myself for remaining hopeful about my outcomes despite what others projected about me. And I say projections because that's exactly what they are. Their own shortcomings encourage them to say hurtful things because if they can get us to believe we can't do better, then we are much more likely to choose them – or someone like them. We are much more likely to settle. I therefore hold men accountable when the women they have been with believe they can't do any better than those men. Nobody actively chooses to diminish or limit themselves. They're often manipulated into doing so.

As for the men who suggested I would never find love, one type of satisfaction I have experienced many times in life is acquiring the very thing people told me was 'unrealistic'. One person's 'unachievable' is another person's 'easy to acquire', and often, the major thing that separates these two people is their mindset. I want you to realise that you *can* be with someone better, and you *will* be with someone better than the person who broke your heart. The world possesses better options, and you are deserving of someone who will not make you doubt your worth.

With this said, I am, of course, a lady of logic as much as I am a woman of abundance, so I wish to address what many of you will likely be thinking now: 'But if we always hope for better and think the grass is greener elsewhere, nobody will settle down or be satisfied.' This is where balance comes in. If you're in a fulfilling relationship with someone who truly loves, respects and cares for you – and you love them in return and are compatible in ways that span from core values to long-term plans – then that is the ultimate goal. That's when you accept someone as your forever. I stopped searching for 'better' when I found my husband because he ticked all those boxes. Anything less than a man who ticks these boxes shouldn't sit at the top of your hierarchy. Even if they may not be the best to someone else, as long as they're YOUR best, that's all that matters. With that said, should your person at the top ever disrespect your relationship, undervalue you or tell you they have fallen out of love for you, then free up that damn space. Back down the rungs of the ladder they go because there will always be someone else who is capable of loving you how you deserve to be loved.

I have an auntie who lives in the United States and she happens to be big on writing lists. Whether it's love-focused lists or career-focused lists, she often reminds my sister and I to write things down to help make them a reality. The power of writing things down is undeniable, and one study which proves this is by *New York Times* bestselling writer and the founder of Leadership IQ, Mark Murphy, titled 'The Gender Gap and Goal-Setting'. It's a study I came across while scrolling through Forbes and it highlighted that people who very vividly describe or picture their goals are anywhere from 1.2 to 1.4 times more likely to successfully accomplish them. This is apparently down to something that goes on in our brain called encoding. 'Encoding is the biological process by which the things we perceive travel to our brain's hippocampus (part of our brain that is responsible for memory), where they're analysed. From there, decisions are made about what gets stored in our long-term memory and, in turn, what gets discarded. Writing improves that encoding process. In other words, when you write it down, it has a much greater chance of being remembered.' Why is this important? Because it's the 'forgetting' that often lands us in trouble. It's the disregarding of key information that will lead us to weaken our boundaries or dismiss our non-negotiables.

When it came to my own post-break-up journeys, there were two lists that helped me greatly. The first was my 'reasons I don't want him' list, and the second was my 'who I actually want' list. And I want you to create both lists today.

So, what should a 'reasons I don't want him' list look like? It's a list that speaks for itself. I want you to write down the reasons you shouldn't want your ex back. Whether it's something that led to your break-up or a character flaw he has, write it down. Here's an example of a past (shortened) 'reasons I don't want him' list I once wrote on an old phone of mine:

- Commitment issues
- Has completely different values from me
- Egocentric at times
- Omits things
- Tests my boundaries
- Not spiritual
- Not as considerate as I would like
- Walks in front of me when we're out together

There were many more lines on my list but for the sake of keeping the example short, you get the drift. It's a valuable exercise because when we're in the midst of loving or missing someone, it's difficult to draw out all the issues and the incompatibilities within the relationship.

'Post-Break-Up Clarity' – also known as PBC – is very real. It's that moment where we suddenly realise all the sh*t we went through. It occurs quite late after a break-up – once the anger, sadness and nostalgia have shifted. But it's an important window because it gives us an opportunity to truly reflect on why we are better off without the other person. If you let this window of opportunity ride out without taking the time out to reflect, then that's when the nostalgia returns. You'll start thinking that someone who was bad for you is actually good for you. You'll start focusing on the few good things they did and will somehow magnify the significance of those things in your head. Don't let your feelings erode reality. If they did anything to undervalue you, write it down and remind yourself that you're better off without them. Remind yourself why *they* should be held accountable for the break-up.

I remember being online and coming across a quote which read, 'If he couldn't tell you he loves you with words, how would you know he does through his actions?' As simple as it might be, it's a question that went viral and set social media on fire. I think its popularity was a result of many women basing the love they receive from their partner largely on words of affirmation over anything else. When you strip away words, it forces you to review how you are truly being treated. For many women who came across this quote, they realised that beyond their partner telling them they care, they do very little to show it. On this basis, I want to ask you the same question. If your ex couldn't verbally tell you that he loved you while he was with you, how would you have known he loved you through his actions? Did his actions reflect someone who valued you or did his actions reflect someone who didn't care?

The second list I want you to write is titled 'the companion I actually want'. For me, this was such a fun list to write because it reenergised me, acting as such a valuable reminder to not settle and take on a hopeful abundance mindset. When you eventually find the person who matches up with your list, it's also such a beautiful feeling. Prior to meeting my husband, I wrote a list detailing the type of life partner I would like to have. I penned the list a year before I met him, and even forgot about it once we met. Two years into our relationship, I was scrolling through my notes app and stumbled upon said list. Imagine my shock when I discovered that my husband ticked absolutely everything on the list. If you're nosey, here's my old list:

- Funny
- Handsome
- Values having a nuclear family
- Taller than me
- Loyal
- Likes travelling
- Believes in monogamy
- Wants to be a husband
- Financially secure
- Intelligent
- Believes in God
- Loved by my family

I was very lucky to have met someone who ticked all my boxes, but to be fair, that's not the case for everyone. Would I have remained with him had he not ticked everything? Of course, because some boxes are bigger than others. For me, his approach to monogamy, his loyalty and his spirituality were non-negotiables, but had he been the same height as me, not very well-travelled or maybe not as financially secure as I would have liked, I wouldn't have disregarded him. I would have chosen him either way. I write all this to say, use your list as a founda- tion and separate your non-negotiables from your negotiables. Know that there is a difference between settling and compromising. Settling is being with someone who possesses your non-negotiable qualities. It's being with someone who doesn't prioritise you or respect you. It's being with someone you are not physically attracted to whatsoever. Compromising is quite different. Your life partner doesn't have to be the 'perfect person'. As amazing as my husband is, he has his flaws, but I'm also not perfect, and we show each other grace because our 'imperfections' don't sit within any non-negotiables.

When you write your own list, write it with an abundance mindset – a hopeful mindset. After a heartbreak at the hands of a f*ck boy, it's easy to assume the world is full of bad guys and that no good guys exist. That's the kind of mindset that will lead you to settling when you don't have to. There are kind, thoughtful, considerate men in this world. They may not all be millionaires or look like Calvin Klein models, but the fact is – you don't have to settle when it comes to being loved and treated with basic respect.

Hold on to your hope with the knowledge that having hope is not naive. If anything, it's a powerful stance to take when it comes to heartbreak recovery, because in having hope, you are asserting that you refuse to let your story be defined by one inconsiderate guy and one difficult chapter in your life. Hope will soften your heart in a way that will have you open to new and wonderful possibilities. It's a f*ck you to the person who hurt you because, in holding on to hope, you are reminding yourself that you are still worthy, still desirable and still capable of embarking on a beautiful love story. Hope is the reminder that genuine and fulfilling love is still out there – even after disappointment.

Acceptance

Before reaching the stage of acceptance on our journey towards healing, we can often assume it's a stage that comes with zero thoughts regarding the past. That's frankly an unnatural level of acceptance. Acceptance isn't about erasing all memory of your previous relationship without a care in the world. It's about accepting the fact you may still think about the past sometimes and your ex may cross your mind on occasion, but in a way that no longer fills you with immeasurable pain. True acceptance is about freedom, it's about zero accountability, it's about not carrying the hurt connected to things that weren't even your fault. After both my heartbreaks,

I eventually got to a place where I carried zero hurt from the past. If, while I was in the thick of those relationships, someone had told me I'd feel completely indifferent in the future, I'd have struggled to believe it, but a willingness to heal, coupled with time passed, can make all the difference. Trust me when I say things will get better and one day you won't be hurting any more.

A big part of accepting your past after a break-up is rebuilding your confidence. A broken heart can really f*ck with your self-esteem, and in the aftermath of a break-up, we can easily forget how amazing we are. Before I share more, I first want to dispel the myth regarding what a confident healing journey looks like. We can often assume that the most confident women deal with break-ups in a very stoic and direct way. We can assume that true confidence is not crying, never feeling ashamed and never worrying about the future. The truth is painful emotions and confidence can co-exist. You can cry to your friends and still feel confident enough to assert a boundary and block your ex, you can worry about the future and still be confident enough to give love a second chance and you can grieve the loss of a past partner while still understanding that you deserve so much better. Confidence after a break-up also doesn't have to be loud. It might seem tempting to prove a point to your ex by posting your hottest selfie, working on a 'revenge body' or rushing back into the dating scene – but true confidence after a break-up is not performative or reactive. It's not preoccupied with how other people perceive your recovery. What matters is about how *you* feel. True confidence is grounded, honest and focused on self. It is liberation. And when you apply confidence after a break-up, you reclaim your identity outside of having a partner in a way that is unconcerned with how they are moving on. In seeing yourself as the prize, you heal in a way that is less preoccupied with how people perceive you and you accept your past with compassion. You understand that the hurt you are recovering from is not your fault and you are not defined by how people choose to treat you.

I see myself as the prize – and I don't mean that I am something to conquer, but rather that I am worthy regardless of anyone's acknowledgement of my worth. People failing to see my value has no impact on how I perceive my value. And therefore, I remain strict regarding what I will and will not accept. Because I am the prize, I set great standards and I am unwilling to accept anything less than the best. Call me delusional if you wish, but developing this mindset has filled me with a strength which has recalibrated how I view betrayal or being undervalued. If someone cannot see that they have lost something good in losing me, then that's their personal problem.

Now, let me explain this in a different way. I want you to view yourself as if you're a blank billion-dollar cheque and your ex is a man who has been handed this great fortune. However, in his ungratefulness and inability to appreciate good things, he carelessly loses the blank cheque. When you assess this scenario, who fumbled? Anyone who now runs into the cheque (you) would be greatly blessed. They'd be thinking, 'Wow! A billion-dollar cheque that just happens to be available. What are the odds?! How lucky am I?!' Furthermore, would you ever beg someone to take a billion-dollar cheque if they acted like it wasn't valuable in the first place? Of course not – because *you* already recognise the value of the cheque, regardless of whether other people do or do not.

Sadly, some women struggle with seeing themselves as the prize – but I believe that's largely down to where they place value. Being a prize isn't about having the perfect face, biggest butt or perkiest boobs. It's not about flexing on your ex, nor is it about being the most desired by men. In fact, it has nothing to do with how others perceive you. Being a prize is about how you see yourself. It's about how your character shows up in the world. If you're a woman who moves with kindness, who doesn't operate with malice, who is committed to personal growth and adding value in the world, then you, my dear, are a prize. Your worth is not up for discussion or negotiation. You don't need a man to validate your existence; you matter simply because you exist.

If you find yourself struggling to feel confident at times, practice finding confidence in your everyday. If you're not someone who typically voices their annoyances, practice speaking up when you'd usually stay quiet. If you're not someone who embarks on things alone, take yourself on a solo date as a challenge. Maybe you would benefit from setting an updated boundary or making a big decision without running to a friend for external validation and support. There are small wins you can undertake which will eventually compound. For me, I gain a lot of confidence in my work – simply advising others and problem solving reminds me of how assertive I can be. My friends also fill me with confidence because they often remind me of how amazing I am. Something as simple as getting dressed in an outfit I love puts a pep in my step. Confidence can be found everywhere. It also grows when we express gratitude. Writing a list of all the things you're grateful for and all the things in yourself that you're proud of is a shortcut to boosting your daily confidence.

Being the prize is very much rooted in zero accountability, because in acknowledging your value, you hold others accountable – not yourself. You are freed from having to justify why you left people or explain why they left you, and you don't feel guilty about being 'too happy' or 'too selfish'. If someone mistreats you, you don't ask, 'What did I do wrong?', instead, you simply acknowledge that they possess bad character and move forward. Reclaiming your confidence on your journey to acceptance isn't about being someone new; it's about being the strongest version of yourself that already exists but was forgotten. And the most powerful part about it is that you don't need anyone's permission to do it. You don't need to be 'chosen' again, because you choose yourself. You don't need 'closure' to be confident, because you find it in yourself. You don't need people to clap for your wins, because you've learnt how to celebrate your wins on your own. And in being confident, you can accept your story free of guilt and self-blame.

Please give yourself permission to be free of the past. You are not defined by your difficult memories. Nor are you responsible for the actions of the person that hurt you. Those memories and actions may have led to your evolution, but you are more than the heartbreak you have experienced. Remember that you don't have to explain anything to anyone on your journey towards finding peace. Find peace in whichever way suits you best – even if you must be a little selfish to do so. Your journey won't look like everyone else's healing journey, and that's okay. Maybe, like me, you will sit with resentment a little longer than you would like to. Maybe you will make some decisions you regret due to nostalgia. So what? Sh*t happens. Heartache makes us do crazy things. Just be kind to yourself in the process. You no longer need to replay conversations in your head, and you definitely don't need to seek answers from any man who has hurt you. You have all the answers you need. You just need to be confident enough to trust yourself.

I hope this book has given you a feeling of acceptance. I hope it's comforted you through all the difficult emotions you may be experiencing at this time – whether that's anger, sadness, shame or loneliness. I also hope that in sharing my personal experiences, I have helped you in some way. My past relationships weren't easy and nor were the break-ups, but the woman I am today is miles stronger than the young woman I was. Heartbreak tested me, shattered me and inevitably encouraged me to put myself back together, but I fortified myself in the process. If I can do it, you can do it too.